You Don't Look Like Someone Who....

Order this book online at www.trafford.com
or email orders@trafford.com

Most Trafford titles are also available at major online book retailers.

Note for Librarians: A cataloguing record for this book is available from Library
and Archives Canada at www.collectionscanada.ca/amicus/index-e.html

Printed in Victoria, BC, Canada.

ISBN: 978-1-4269-0425-7 (sc)

*Our mission is to efficiently provide the world's finest, most comprehensive book publishing
service, enabling every author to experience success. To find out how to publish your
book, your way, and have it available worldwide, visit us online at www.trafford.com*

Trafford rev. 9/1/2009

www.trafford.com

North America & international
toll-free: 1 888 232 4444 (USA & Canada)
phone: 250 383 6864 • fax: 812 355 4082

Contents

Acknowledgements

This book truly would not have come into being without the many contributions of friends and relatives. Some shared their technical expertise in helping me to acquire the computer skills necessary to write these memoirs: others encouraged me to dare to believe that some people might be interested in vicariously sharing some of my European experiences.

Chief among these cherished friends and relatives is my cousin Dauphine Walker-Shivers, a role model whose accomplishments include several firsts in our family: our first college graduate; our first PhD; our first college professor; and our first teacher for the Department of Defense Dependent Schools (DoDDS). She inspired me to become a part of the DoDDS system and later suggested that I write these memoirs of living and traveling in Europe.

I owe thanks to Larry Burner, a former Frankfurt American High School (FAHS) colleague who, in the early days of computer courses in public schools, introduced me to the world of computers by allowing me to sit in on one of his high school computer classes.

Dr. Toby Levine, professor of the class Black Women Writers, suggested that one of the essays I wrote was worthy of publication. Her offer to give me contact information of publishers was the seed that after many years grew into my writing of the memoirs.

A very special friend to whom I will be forever grateful is Ruby Speight, who demystified the computer for me as she sat patiently by my side, helping me to learn to navigate this alien world. Her teaching was so effective that I now can assist others with basic computer functions.

Myron Kern, another esteemed colleague and friend, showed incredible kindness in never making me feel dense as he used lunch time to assist me with seemingly endless computer problems.

Veneka Pussewela, yet another colleague and friend, gave me a book of publication information at a time when I was at a standstill, not knowing how to get started with the publication. On a couple of occasions when lack of computer ability sent me into a panic, she made "house calls" in order to assist me.

Even with all the computer help I received, I could never get the charts right. For that, I turned to Danielle McBride, a friend and technical expert par excellence who also spent some of her lunch time to help me.

I am indebted to Tasha Jones, colleague, opera pal, and all-round friend, for sending information about the publishing house I eventually chose and for her generosity in my getting the equipment needed for technically producing the manuscript.

Tony Spatola, the brilliant chairman of the English department, indirectly helped me to write my memoirs, for his hiring me years ago to join the adjunct faculty enabled me to take computer classes and provided the place for the many hours of practice I needed to overcome my fear of all things technological. More than that, though, I am deeply thankful to him for showing confidence in my abilities as an educator and writer.

To Barbara Elzy-Boz, Sadie Fairley, Audrey Haynes, Evelyn Alston Jude, Geraldine Purnell, and Robert Stevenson, I owe special thanks, for they were participants in some of the madcap occurrences written about in these memoirs.

To **all** my friends and well-wishers who offered encouragement to a fledging memoirist, I give unending thanks.

Preface

One day in 2007, I was enjoying a conversation with an Italian American colleague I had just met. Both of us had lived and traveled in foreign countries. As we talked briefly of places we had seen and of plans to write about our travels, she said, "You don't look like someone who has traveled a lot." Only after I returned home did I think about the incongruity of that remark. What did it mean? What does a person who has traveled a lot look like?

Evidently, I don't "look like" a lot of things. I don't "look like someone who" enjoys the opera. I don't "look like someone who" understands foreign languages. I don't "look like someone who" frequents museums, appreciates the sanctity and beauty of cathedrals, or is moved by the pathos of Rossini's *Petite Messe Solennelle*. I say this because I get many comments from people who are surprised to learn that I do. Why? Like many, I'm the product of an American culture that values education, the arts, beautiful things, and travel. Because I enjoy these things, people say, "You're different." Different from whom? From other African Americans? That is a remark often addressed to those of us who don't fit the stereotype. I know scores of people who enjoy the same things that I do, who speak Standard English, who speak other languages, who have advanced degrees, and who travel throughout the world—in short, regular people who are living middle-class lives.

I guess I look so little like someone who speaks a European language that in my presence some people feel free to say things in their language that they wouldn't ordinarily say publicly. For example, one summer my friend Audrey, an African American living and teaching in Germany, visited me here in New Jersey. One of the touristy things we did was to visit Constitution Hall and the Liberty Bell. As we waited in line, we overheard a German conversation in which the woman spoke disparagingly of one of the guards. When she referred to his "big belly," Audrey and I said to each other, "Should we?" We couldn't resist. Turning to the couple, we said in clear German: "*Willkommen in den USA. Sie kommen aus Deutschland, stimmt? Wie lange sind Sie hier?*" Astonishment and embarrassment caused them to freeze momentarily: it was as though they had been caught *in flagrante delicto* in some very private act. Who would have thought that those two brown people, Audrey and I, could understand the whole German conversation, especially in a country so far away? I absolutely loved it! Maybe I should suggest to the FBI that I'd be an asset to them. I could possibly make a good spy because few people would ever suspect me of "looking like someone who…" (The reader can fill in the blank.)

Introduction

In writing these memoirs of my travels and studies abroad during my twenty-three years in Germany, I leave a legacy of memories to my nieces Dedara and Pamela and my nephew DeAndre so that they can know something about Tante, who for many years lived far away and visited only occasionally. I hope that the richness of my experiences will serve to show them, other young African Americans, and members of other minorities that they too can experience such and much more.

I had never really thought of writing about these experiences with a view to sharing them with the public. But, a few months before she died, my cousin Dauphine urged me to do so in order to encourage others to know that they could share in the beauties of the earth. While I was still in undergraduate school, Dauphine went to France to teach in the DoDDS system. She often suggested that I do the same.

At the close of school one year, the summer threatened to be as bleak and as full of loneliness as the previous one had been (disappointment in a relationship). But from somewhere deep inside came a spark of defiance and self-protection. I would **not** sit by the whole summer and allow myself to be swallowed up in misery. I thought: "What can I do to take care of **ME**, of my well-being? What can I do that would be totally out of the ordinary, something I have never dreamed of doing?" I decided to take a trip. At the travel agency, I had no plans, no idea where I wanted to go. When the agent suggested a cruise, I was delighted. From Chicago I flew to New York to board the S.S. *Homeric* for fourteen days of cruising the Caribbean Isles. And that was the beginning of my determination to see the world. After many years of teaching in the States, in August 1972 I finally took my cousin's advice: I applied to teach in Europe for the Department of Defense Dependent Schools (DoDDS).

When I told colleagues and acquaintances about my acceptance into the program, I was met with the same dissuasion some people employ with those who dare to venture something out of the ordinary. One woman even asked: "What are you running away from?" Thank God for the strength to resist opposition and to follow my dream. I was the traveler in Robert Frost's "The Road Not Taken":

> Two roads diverged in a yellow wood,
> And sorry I could not travel both
> [...]
> I took the one less traveled by,
> And that has made all the difference.

And what a difference that has been!

Author's Notes about the Class Essays

The pleasures of living overseas included opportunities to study in other countries. Some of the studies were sponsored by DoDDS (the Department of Defense Dependent Schools). To enhance our writing programs, DoDDS brought professors from various State-side colleges and universities to conduct workshops for its teachers in Europe. Because the assignments were catalysts for my writing this book, I have included some. Though the incidents in a couple of the essays occurred before my going to Europe, I have included them because remembering them evoked memories of wonderful and unique experiences enjoyed there. For example, the essay about my art teacher's remorse at his hurting words in undergraduate school made me see that many of my dreams were realized in Europe. The essay about the diva caused me to recall the joy experienced in singing on some of the opera stages (as a member of the chorus) and in churches in Europe.

Other studies were done simply for the delight of learning: for example, courses in the study of German, Italian, and Spanish. Because I was in proximity to lands where these languages are spoken, I had opportunities to do more than read about them: I could also use them in my interactions with the native speakers.

CHAPTER I

Living in Germany

In August 1972, my dream of living and working overseas became a reality: I was assigned to teach at Frankfurt American High School for dependants of military personnel. At Fort Sheridan, Illinois, several African American educators recruited from the Chicago area arrived for processing. A woman handling our processing expressed surprise at the unprecedented number of African Americans being processed at one time. I didn't know the reason then but later discovered it. Because of the diversity of its overseas military population, the government had seen the need to diversify its educational staff. Thus, we were sent to various schools in Europe.

After an eight-hour flight, a plane-load of African American educators descended on Frankfurt, some to stay there and others to go on to other parts of Europe. We were taken by teacher-greeters to the dormitory of Frankfurt American High School, where we stayed overnight. FAHS, my school, was on a post right in the *Innenstadt* (interior of Frankfurt). In addition to the school, the area contained the headquarters for V Corps, the Officers' Club, the community library, the chapel, the dining hall, and a few houses for the big brass. I had wanted to be assigned to Spain, but I soon realized that Germany was ideal. It's a beautiful country, with awe-inspiring mountains, legendary rivers, renowned wines, beloved operas, impressive castles, and bustling metropolitan areas.

For the first years I lived in a section of town near the American hospital. After I had lived for five years in a military BOQ (Bachelor Officers' Quarters) in Frankfurt, the government allowed single personnel to move out onto the Economy (the German areas that were not part of the American enclaves of housing, shops, movie theaters, chapels, schools, and hospitals). Living in the BOQ wasn't bad: I had two rooms, a bath, and access to a common kitchen down the hall. Still, I was pleased over the prospect of moving to a German area. I had come to Germany to experience German life and culture, and living on the Economy was key to doing so.

In lovely Schoenberg, a section of Kronberg am Taunus, a town at the foot of the Taunus Mountains about fifteen miles from Frankfurt, I lived in a spacious apartment owned by the Hessische Stiftung, a foundation connected with the family who had once owned the historic Schloss Kronberg. The castle had been converted into the Schlosshotel Kronberg. On my way home from church, I sometimes treated myself to breakfast at **my** castle. Sometimes on Saturdays as my apartment was being cleaned, Audrey came up from Frankfurt to join me for breakfast or afternoon tea in the castle. We loved occasionally playing ladies of leisure and affluence. Actually, we weren't really play-acting: the government provided well for us. It paid our rent, allowed us to travel home every two years at government expense, allowed us to shop tax-free in German businesses, and gave us discounts on foreign hotels and travel. Thus, our lifestyle allowed certain luxuries that we could scarcely afford on our own.

In the beginning I felt guilty about having someone to clean my apartment: it seemed the height of affectation. However, I was actually quite busy: German, Spanish, and Italian lessons; voice lessons; travel; church work; and teaching duties. Thus, I had little time for or interest in cleaning house. Having financed a part of my under-grad work by cleaning other people's houses, I had paid my dues. So Saturday was indeed a day of earned leisure.

CHAPTER II

Travel Highlights

From Ships to Trains

W hen I was a very young child living at 1501 Minnie Street in north Memphis, I often heard the nightly sounds of a distant train. Those sounds filled me with an intense, though vague, longing for something I could not name, for my experiences were limited to the few Black neighborhoods where I had grown up. I didn't know enough about the world beyond to know what it was that the sounds evoked in me. I could sense, though, that the train was going somewhere **far** away from my mundane world. Somehow those sounds of a world far away seemed related to the fairy tales I listened to and inhabited every Saturday morning with *Let's Pretend*, a radio show. As I passed from one grade to the next, my awareness of the world outside grew. It was in third grade that I began to connect the train whistles and *Let's Pretend* with the distant lands I was learning about in the curriculum's songs: "Ma come, come, come bella bimba" (Italian); "Ar hyd y nos" (Welsh); and "Solomon Levi" (Jewish). I knew neither the lands nor the meanings of the words, but I loved their mystical, fascinating sounds, and I longed to see the lands where they were spoken. I have never lost that fascination with exotic lands and people.

As an adult many years later, I learned that "whatever the mind can image [picture], it can achieve." However, at that young age and with no experience of any distant lands or people, I could not imagine that I would ever see such people or hear such languages. Certainly I never thought that I would one day travel to many parts of the world. It would be years before either of those desires came to fruition. Yet, I would travel not only on those whistle-tooting trains but also on planes, ferries, and ocean liners.

Recalling the many lands I have been blessed to see fills me with that same sense of awe that I felt as a child. With much gratitude, I have compiled a list of the many waters I have sailed upon. This book of memoirs briefly discusses some of my travels "by land and by sea." Maybe these memoirs will help some other "disadvantaged" child to know that the world is his or hers to experience.

Memorable Ship Travels

Alexandria, Egypt

In 1972, when the planeload of newly recruited African American teachers arrived in Germany, we were given pamphlets describing the shock we could expect in meeting for the first time a culture different from our own. However, through music, cuisine, and language study, I was already familiar with some aspects of Western European culture. Therefore, I didn't experience culture shock in any of those countries: my first experience of culture shock was in Alexandria, Egypt.

When I was a college student, I used to watch *Omnibus*, a TV program which featured distant lands and cultures, and for those of us who could not afford exotic travel, this program brought all kinds of wonders vicariously into our lives. On the program I saw the land of the pharaohs, the Sphinx, the pyramids. Of course, I had never seen any place other than Memphis, Tennessee. And now years later I would see Memphis, Egypt, where I would experience true culture shock.

My good friend Audrey and I had driven to Heidelberg, where we boarded a bus for Ancona, Italy, from which we sailed to Alexandria (not on a luxury liner, but on a cargo ship with space for a limited number of passengers). The ship had only basic amenities; still it was adequate. One night's entertainment featured a "dance contest." One of the few passengers in the little room, an Italian man, dragged an unwilling Audrey onto the dance floor. It was really funny because Audrey is rather reluctant to call undue attention to herself. So, in order to avoid further notice by continuing to refuse, she approached the tiny dance space perfunctorily. Still, they won a nominal trophy, which Audrey discarded as soon as she was out of her partner's sight.

In Alexandria the tour guide tried to prepare us for Egypt. But no words could prepare us for our first encounter with a culture having one foot in antiquity and the other in the twilight zone. Never had I seen such seeming chaos; so much moving, shouting humanity; so many cars and donkey-drawn carts vying for space in the streets; such honking of horns; such erratic driving. NOISE was the name of Alexandria. Yet, it was hypnotic. Later, a bus drove us to Cairo, which was more of the same. Mosques, souks, people in varying shades of browns, shouts of "Welcome home!"—absolutely fascinating!

This trip to Egypt was very short, but it whetted my desire to return. And I did—several times.

From Southampton, England (on the *QE2*) To New York

From Frankfurt's *Bahnhof* to London's Waterloo Train Station to Southampton's port, Audrey and I set out in great style for our home leave in the summer of 1993: we had booked passage on the most luxurious ocean liner afloat—the *QE2*. In Southampton, we unknowingly stayed at a bed and breakfast run by one of the employees of the ship. The next morning when we went to the pier where the ship was berthed, we discovered that our landlady was one of the people checking the passengers in. Seeing us, she allowed us to embark hours before the official embarkation, so much so that by the time the other passengers arrived, we had already showered and taken a long nap. That was only the beginning of a first-class experience.

The *QE2* avoided the designation of first and second classes. Instead, the class of the stateroom was indicated by the name of the restaurant to which the passenger was assigned. We assumed that we had second class rooms (Mauritania restaurant). But the steward took us through corridors leading to the Columbia restaurant (first class). We were surprised. You see, our government's arrangement with Cunard Lines was simply the guarantee of a space. The class depended on the ship's situation. Because this was mid-June, a few days before high season, there were empty staterooms. Therefore, the ship gave us first class accommodations. I must mention that there were levels of first class: we were at the bottom. Still, it was absolute luxury. As often happened, Audrey and I seemed to be the **Only Ones**. In fact, however, at the end of the trip, we saw some more of **Us**. They wanted to know where we had been for the five and a half days it had taken to cross the Atlantic. As members of the band, they were in second class. Audrey later said that, while first class had its good points, one negative was that at tea time a waiter served us and we were too embarrassed to take as many cookies as we wanted. Also, our fellow passengers in first class were little British dowagers and their companions, so everything moved slowly and quietly. I loved it!

There was no lack of things to do: the ship was a mini-city. It had a laundry, florist, cinema, chapel, library, spa and health club, beauty salon, bank, pools, casinos, nine bars, five restaurants, fourteen TV and radio stations, Harrods, and other boutiques. But I had just finished a year of trying to show high school students the merits of avoiding dangling participles and split infinitives. Many of the students had resisted my efforts to instill in them the love of homework. My struggles to lead them out of the darkness of ignorance into the light of knowledge had taken a lot out of me. Therefore, I was tired. I wanted no partying: I simply wanted to sleep without having to make my bed, eat without cooking, read, watch closed circuit television, go to an occasional movie, watch the moonlight on the ocean, and feel the presence of the Supreme Being.

The sailing across the Atlantic took five and a half days. To avoid the "jet lag" resulting from a time difference of six hours, every night the captain had us to set our watches back one hour when traveling westward and one hour ahead when traveling to England.

This transatlantic crossing was the first of my five.

Across Europe by Rail

Lands I have crossed by rail are too numerous to be fully recounted here. For that reason, I'll briefly discuss those that I consider especially memorable.

From Frankfurt, Germany to Torremolinas and Andalusia, Spain

How annoying it must be to be truly beautiful! During my first trip to Spain via EurailPass, I got a taste of how the beautiful must feel in having so much attention directed towards them.

From Frankfurt, I was traveling to Torremolinas, Spain, where I would join my cousin Hazel and her Chicago teachers' group. The trip began uneventfully enough, but when the train reached Irun, Spain (the French-Spanish border), things changed. Suddenly on the platform, there was a big commotion. Train personnel were announcing the presence of "La Morena! La Morena!" Looking to see the cause of the commotion, I found all eyes on me: **I** was La Morena (the dark one, the Moor: I'm not sure what the literal translation of the term is, but it referred to me.) That was only the beginning. While I was planning to see Europe, I had no idea that Europe would want to see **me.**

In Spain, as I sat at meals, often I would look up to find kitchen staff staring at me through the tiny glass of kitchen doors. Coming from Chicago, where I had passed anonymously through throngs of people, I was amazed to discover that I was a big attraction in the Spanish (and other European) towns I visited.

Earlier, I mentioned experiencing some of the attention the beautiful receive. Actually, I didn't credit the inordinate amount of attention I received in Spain to any great beauty of mine. (I knew better. Years of being invisible in the States had taught me that.) Rather, it was the unusual aspect of my appearance and the unexpectedness of my appearing in little towns. In towns of 5'4" Caucasians, a 5'10" African American woman traveling alone was indeed a rarity.

After I joined my cousin's group for tours around the Costa del Sol, we spent some days in Morocco. When my cousin left, I remained alone to explore Spain. And that's when the attention intensified. One pale tourist pursued me so much that I would look up and down the streets before venturing from my hotel. Going out for ice cream became a chore. Walking down the street was sure to bring unwanted stares from people sitting at outside tables. I complained to the Caucasian woman of a mixed race couple I'd met that the unwanted attention was making me very uncomfortable. As we walked through the gardens of the Alhambra, one of the guards came up to me and put his arm around me. Funny her remark: "They'll flirt with just anybody." I honestly became tired of having no privacy to explore the towns. On a local train in a little Spanish town, when I complained to a North African woman living in Spain that I found it annoying to have so much unwanted attention, she said, "Maybe it's the way you carry yourself." As I was protesting that I didn't do anything improper, a Spanish soldier sitting in front of us turned around and caught my necklace (near my **bosom**) and examined it—while I was wearing it! I said to her: "See?"

Once in Andalusia I met two English-speaking Spaniards who took me to dinner and a nightclub inside a cave. Although the setting was different, almost everything else was typical of nightclubs around the world. Some of the music was Spanish, and some universal. It was a fun evening with flamenco, tapas, sangria, and social dancing. But, when we returned to the city and A had left, B made an odd proposal for his friend. According to B, his friend had told him to ask me whether I would consider staying with B for a while so that A could visit me there. The reputed reason that A wanted me to stay with his friend was that he (A) lived with his mother and couldn't let me stay with him. It was a surprising offer because there had been no indication that anyone was thinking of such. Of course, I thanked him for his offer of hospitality and returned to my hotel. The next day I continued my travels through Andalusia.

As I was returning to Germany from another trip to Spain, the connecting train from Torremolinos to Madrid was five hours late, causing me to arrive in Madrid around midnight. Thus, I had missed my connecting train to Paris. I wasn't too worried because I thought I'd wait in the station until early morning, when the next train would arrive. But no, that was not to be. The station locked up every night from midnight until 6 am. What was I to do? Where was I to go? I had no hotel reservation; in fact, I didn't know of any hotel in the area or in any other part of Madrid. I didn't know Madrid. And I knew only basic Spanish. ("Where is the library?" "What's your name?" "What time does the next train leave?" Things like that.)

Feeling almost overwhelmed by panic, I approached a station guard and asked for help. He was most eager to *ayudarme*. He asked whether I'd care to walk down a couple of blocks to a nearby bar and have something to drink. Well, I had been on a hot, dusty train for many hours and was indeed thirsty. Off we headed toward the bar. (People who are more circumspect might censure me for my apparent naiveté in going off with a stranger and at midnight. But he was a policeman, for goodness sakes, and if policemen can't be trusted, who can?) Anyway, in spite of the late hour, there were many people milling about in the streets. So there was no danger, and I was so looking forward to a nice cold Coke. As we walked along, he looked furtively around and whispered something about our being *juntos*.

It took a while before I realized that *juntos* meant "together" and that he was not talking about **walking** together. As I looked down at his gun in the holster, fatigue vanished and animal craft took over. I told him that the prospect of being *juntos* was very appealing, but at the moment I was tired, dirty, and sweaty. I would meet him the next morning. He agreed, and we walked downstairs where I ducked into a washroom and lost him. After an hour I came out and went in another direction.

Another employee at the station told me that across the street at the clinic for the railway was someone who spoke English. And indeed there was. Two of the men who worked there greeted me with open arms (how open I was soon to find out). They brought me cold chicken, wine, and fruit. We sat outside and talked for hours. And I thought it wouldn't be too bad to sit and talk until the station opened again. But one of the men had a better idea, it seemed. All of the employees at the clinic worked a certain number days on and then off. That meant that each had a mini apartment. The one who was especially friendly invited me to while away the time in his room where we would talk until train time. How lovely! We went to his room and I sat in a big comfortable chair. Noticing my exhaustion, the nice man invited me to sit on the bed, all the while assuring me that it was quite safe to do so. So I did. We talked some more. Then he invited me to lean back and just relax. Heck! I was tired and the bed very inviting. As I started to lean back, I felt an arm gently slipping beneath my back. Uh, oh! I sat up as he began to talk of kissing my irresistible lips. There I was—alone in the room with someone who wanted to kiss me because he "had never kissed an African American before." I assured him that we were no different from other women. But he wasn't convinced. So I had to promise to meet him in a few days after I had gone to some fictitious somewhere or the other. He was really a nice man, but I think that the opportunity that had fallen into his lap (bed) was such a rare and unexpected one that he felt he had to act upon it. For the next several hours, speaking with him in a mixture of English and very badly broken Spanish, I managed to divert his interest from *el amor* to language. When morning finally came, he walked with me to the station as proudly as if he were escorting a queen. Well, that was certainly a new experience for me: no one in the States had ever appeared honored to be with me.

Finally, I was on my way to Germany via France. By the time I boarded the train to Paris, it was night. As I usually did, I chose an unoccupied compartment so that I could stretch out. As I was enjoying a much appreciated nap, the compartment door opened and in walked (and sat) a French conductor. After a bit of small talk, he asked whether I had ever kissed a Frenchman. (Noticing my reluctance to carry on a conversation, he asked whether I was afraid of the French. He said that if I answered "yes," he would leave. Naturally I said that I feared the French, so he left and I slept. In Verdi's opera *Don Carlos*, the heroine bemoans her fatal beauty: "O, don fatale." Sound familiar? It went on like that: on trains, in train stations, in restaurants, in castles.

But such notice wasn't limited to Spain: it was much of southern Europe. For example, once in Siracusa, an auto followed me, and when I reached the end of a street, it had driven down a parallel one and was waiting for me at the end of the block. Once in an Italian town, I was looking at a window display which consisted of only an arrangement of white sheets. Trying to see how I could achieve the same effect in my apartment, I stood many minutes mentally turning the sheets about. Seeing me staring at apparently nothing, a man walked up and whispered: "*Quanto?*" (How much?)

On a train somewhere in Spain, again exhausted I chose an empty compartment so that I could doze in the sun, undisturbed by chatter. After a while the sound of an opening door woke me as a young man entered. He sat quietly in the seat facing me, and I went back to sleep. A short time later, I was awakened by a touch on my knee. He had moved over so that he was almost directly in front of me. He politely asked: "*Puedo tocarLe?*" ("May I touch you?") After replying "No," I thought him harmless enough and went back to sleep. Some time later, I was again awakened by a touch on my knee: "*Quiere tocarme?*"

After asking whether I wanted to touch him, he politely showed me where he was inviting me to touch him. Indignant (but not scared) I said: "No, and if you don't stop bothering me, I'm going to call the conductor." He thought over that possibility as the train came to a halt. Then he gently said: "*Voy a tocarLe y voy corriendo*." (I'm going to touch you and I'm going to run.") **And he did!** A gentle tap on my bosom. Before I could react, he hopped off the train and went scurrying down the platform.

Another time–this time somewhere in France–I was again the lone occupant of a train compartment. Distracted from my book, I noticed an odd movement outside the door of the compartment. His arm moving rhythmically up and down, a man was grinning foolishly at me and masturbating. I had learned that flashers and others of that ilk derive pleasure from the outraged reactions of the observer. Therefore, I denied him that satisfaction: I calmly returned to my book and gave absolutely no reaction. (Because the car was well-lit and full of passengers, I wasn't afraid.)

Still another time—somewhere in Italy–Barbara and I had a compartment to ourselves. (I had quickly dispatched the two men who had invited themselves in for conversation. Enough is enough!) Later Barbara left the compartment. When she hadn't returned after a couple of hours, I didn't worry. She certainly wasn't lost: the train hadn't stopped. Finally, when the train did stop, Barbara appeared about five minutes later: she had been stuck in the washroom. Nobody had heard her yells for help because of the clickety-clack of the train. It was only at the stop that she could make herself heard. As she told what had happened, the expression on her face warned me to keep very quiet and still until it was safe to talk. During the two hours that she had been screaming and sweating and inhaling noxious fumes, I had been comfortably reading. Civility was difficult for her at that moment.

After receiving so much attention as I traveled through Europe, on a subconscious level I began to believe that I was irresistible, if not to all, at least to many European men. I believed it so much that any time a man looked in my direction, I was sure he wanted to get to know me. In fact, once while I was waiting for a train in a small Italian town, two men approached me and said something in Italian. By this time, a belief in my own charms and an overexposure to several languages in a short time convinced me that they were flirting. Well, I was having none of that! I told them in a hodgepodge of Italian, German, and Spanish (all rudimentary) that I had other plans and thus was not interested. The men looked at each other in astonishment. One said, "I just wanted to know when the next train leaves." How easily we delude ourselves.

After many such escapades in southern Europe, I arrived safe but spent at my apartment in lovely Schoenberg, Germany. Some time later I was ready to go north.

From Frankfurt, Germany to Copenhagen, Denmark

What was especially interesting about this, one of my many train trips throughout Western Europe, was that en route to Scandinavia I awoke from a nap and saw portholes. Portholes on a train! Since European train travel was still new to me, I had not realized that some trains boarded ferries. After a while, I decided to leave the train and go down the stairs to explore the ferry. I had no idea that there were several trains aboard the ferry and that there were different levels. So shortly before we were due to reach land, I found that I was lost. I had wandered about the ferry without taking note of the section where my train was. Again a moment of panic. All my things were on a train that I could not find. Of course, as in so many cases of an "innocent abroad," I was saved just in time.

From Denmark to Narvik, Norway

On another trip to Scandinavia, I met Roslyn, a music teacher from Australia. This train ride took us north of the Arctic Circle to one of the northernmost train stops in the world. Some of the marvels of this ride included seeing mountain lakes in the distance, passing fjords and waterfalls, and experiencing daylight at midnight.

On the train one morning I woke to sounds of Roslyn playing the flute. As I looked out the window of the compartment, I saw distant mountain lakes shrouded in mist. The combination of nature's still beauty and the haunting sounds of the flute had a mystical quality that made this trip especially memorable. Arriving at midnight with no reservations or names of hotels, we didn't know where we'd spend the night. As we were preparing to sleep in the doorway of a closed shop, a police car came by. The officers drove us to a clean, newly constructed youth hostel with a lake in back. The accommodations were plain but clean and economical. And there was an abundance of good food.

From Moscow (Russia) to Vladivostok (Siberia) on the *Trans Siberian Express*

The very sound of the name *Trans Siberian Express* conjured up all kinds of images: crossing a forbidden continent; seeing races of people seldom seen in the West; hearing a language that had no relationship to any other that I had heard; meeting present-day counterparts of exotic characters like Doctor Zhivago, Boris Goudonov, and Prince Igor with the Polovetsian Maidens. This train ride was the most beautiful, the most pleasant of all my train travel. It was full of superlatives: the longest train ride in the world (six and a half days from Moscow to Vladivostok); the largest forest in the world, the Siberian Taiga, where we were treated to a royal picnic; and the deepest lake in the world, Lake Baikal, where we sailed for a few hours on cerulean water that, as the root of the word shows, was truly heavenly.

Greece

On Monday night, 10 July 1979, one event in the Theater of Herodotus Atticus (on the side of the Acropolis) was the Bamberg Symphony Orchestra with Eda Moser, soprano, performing works of Berlioz, R. Strauss, and Brahms. That was one of the most glorious experiences of my life. It was a combination of many things. First, it was the awe of being in a venerated theater of 161 A.D. Sitting under the stars and feeling the presence of the thousands who had enjoyed activities there, I was ready to accept with acclaim even a mediocre performance. How stirring, then, was this stellar program! The soprano sang so clearly, so smoothly, so effortlessly that the music seemed actually to flow from her. I'm not especially fond of Berlioz, Brahms, or Strauss, but Eda Moser's voice revealed extreme beauty—so much so that when I returned to Frankfurt I bought a recording of her doing works by these composers.

Aboard the *Adriadne*, Tuesday evening

It was unbelievable, like something in a book. I was aboard a ferry—the *Adriadne*—heading from Piraeus to Crete. Like most of the other tourists, I decided to go as cheaply as possible, so I had a (can you believe it?) fourth-class ticket. I was down in the hold of the ship with a thousand others—some tourists but mostly locals. I think they were trying to outdo each other with the noise volume. Children were crying—some really; others were making the sounds of pseudo crying, which demands that desires be satisfied. Adults were calling down the corridor to each other. Male voices were booming as the men made themselves heard by others standing at toes' end from them. A human sound conspicuously lacking was that of a parent telling the children to "cease and desist."

As I entered a women's toilet, the other females (short, pale, gold-toothed and clothed all over in long black dresses) looked with hostility and suspicion at me, a tall, African American woman with a very short Afro and in jeans. Finally, one of their men came over and asked: "Are you a man or a woman?" When I answered, "A woman: what are you?" he swelled up in indignation.

I determined to try for some much-needed sleep. The night before, I had slept fewer than six hours. I had been sightseeing, had seen a concert, and then had gone to a restaurant. This morning I got up early to meet Alfonso, a nice guy from Columbia, to sightsee, to go to Piraeus, and then to catch a ship to Crete. So there I was on board the *Ariadne*.

Crete

Early on the morning of 11 July 1979, we docked at Iraklion, Crete, known as the cradle of European civilization (not of civilization in general, as the guidebooks say). I was the typical tourist: looking in windows, gesturing wildly, grunting, pointing to myself, acting out a charade that left everyone frustrated.

Later, I went to the outskirts of Iraklion—Knossos, the capital of the ancient Minoan civilization. There I walked through labyrinthine ruins of palaces. In Iraklion itself, there is an archeological museum housing several sarcophagi of the Minoans. They were extremely short people. The sarcophagi looked as if they were three feet or less: they seemed to be half my height. Even one of the local guides remarked on the short stature of the Minoans.

On board the *Ariadne* returning to Piraeus. 11 July 1979: Wednesday evening, around 6 pm.

I must regretfully say that I am disappointed with Greece—today's Greece, that is. All of its greatness seems to belong only to the past. Archeological monuments aside, Greece is a most dismal place: a dry, barren, rocky, dusty terrain. Dirty, trash-strewn cities and villages— junk heaps and other eyesores right on the main roads. Worst of all, though, are the people—at least the ones with whom the tourist must come in contact: museum ticket sellers, sellers of museum brochures, train conductors, clerks at tourist centers, sellers of boat tickets—in short, the people whose livelihood is connected with tourism. They scream at tourists; scowl, growl, let loose a volley of invectives when checking Eurail and Interrail passes; and give abrupt answers at tourist centers. They treat tourists of all nationalities, ages, and sexes with equal contempt. Of all of the nationalities I have met in my traveling,

I would award the nastiness medal to the Greeks. Of all people—the Greeks! I had thought that they were so noble, so warm, so cultured. I had been so fascinated with them through an earlier encounter that I was inspired to come to Europe to live. Ah well! It was my erroneous thinking. I should have known better: it is as wrong to generalize about the good of a whole group as it is about the bad. I've observed that the Greeks are rude not only to foreigners but also to each other. I've seen several instances of altercations involving table-slapping, finger-jabbing men who seemed on the verge of physical attack.

Athens

I arrived in Athens early on Thursday, 12 July 1979, from Crete. By the time I arrived at the train station to make arrangements for leaving on the last train to Thessaloniki, it was too late to take any day trips. At the train station, I encountered two unprovoked cases of rudeness from those whose job it is to serve travelers: a ticket seller and a waiter. I was totally baffled. I'm ashamed to say that a few tears fell, of course out of sight of the m.f.s.* I almost decided to leave Greece right away, but I planned to hold out for another two days. I determined to come to Greece never again. (No, it's not what a person might think: it's **malefactors**.)

Kavala, Greece, a few days later.

From Thessaloniki, I took a local bus north to Kavala. The ride was harrowing because we were riding at an elevation overlooking the Aegean Sea. Yet the sea was so beautiful that it made up for the rudeness of the people. I didn't leave Greece until much later: I had met my own "Zorba," a Greek seaman, for another of my unforgettable romantic episodes. My impressions of Greece are altogether different now.

From Frankfurt, Germany to Istanbul, Turkey

What an inauspicious beginning for a trip! In midwinter Audrey and I took a train from Frankfurt to Istanbul. We had booked a sleeper because the trip would take about three days, but the first sight of the train filled us with apprehension. It was East European, not German. It was old, dirty, and packed with humanity. Loaded with gifts, *Gastarbeiter* from Yugoslavia, Bulgaria, and Turkey were returning home for the Christmas holidays. Because the doors were filled with people jostling to get on the train to grab unreserved spots in the corridors, gifts were being shoved through the windows: small refrigerators, TVs, trunks. Since the corridors were filled with people who had no seats, Audrey and I struggled to get through to our compartment. As I stepped into the compartment, I was shoved backward by a big, oily-looking man. Well, of course, I began shouting at the burly, uncouth someone with whom we would spend the next three days in close quarters. Once we were in, I spotted the sleeping conditions. In my many travels I had learned that, in order to afford extensive travel, I had to relegate temporarily to the deepest recesses of my mind all desires for the government-afforded sumptuousness of my lifestyle. But the sight of that drab, scratchy-looking woolen blanket and those dingy sheets was distressing. I determined that under no circumstances would that unappetizing combination ever touch my skin.

In addition to the uncouth man, Audrey, and me, the compartment included the boor's adult son and another woman, who slept prone for two days, forcing me to remain lying down in my bunk above her.

At some point, Nature called all the compartment mates. To answer, I stepped out into the corridor crowded with people who had no reservations and thus no seats. Heading for the toilet, I pressed through the throng of people flashing their gold teeth in friendly smiles. After a seeming eternity, I reached the toilet, only to find it occupied by a massive, immovable Rock of Gibraltar, her snores a

"Do-not-disturb" warning sign. Back I went past my compartment to the toilet at the other end, which was available but should have had a sign: "Use at your own peril."

When I returned to the compartment, Audrey had a strange look on her face as she whispered: "The nasty thing!" Well, while the son and I were outside struggling to get through the packed humanity, the father answered Nature's call in his own way. He drank the contents of a can of soda, urinated into it, emptied it out the train's window, and then repeated the process two more times! I do hope that the wind was right and that poor Audrey was spared the further indignity of being splattered by alien urine. However, I suppose the boor really ought to be admired for his ingenuity.

I made it without a blanket through most of the night. But it was freezing in the compartment: the heater wasn't working. I gave in and used the blanket. (I try not to think about it.)

Cold and the Call weren't the only problems: we were famished. You see, before we left Frankfurt, I had told Audrey of my plans to fix a BIG lunch. But no! Audrey didn't always agree with my homey approach to things like sleeping on the ground in an Oslo park while rain fell; or traveling fourth class on a ferry on the Aegean Sea; or staying in a ½ star hotel in Amsterdam, where the resident monkey grabbed my sweater as I passed by in the breakfast room; or staying in a cheap hotel in Madrid, where it was so cold that four of us had to sleep in one bed and under our coats. No, she had to insist on first-class travel: we would eat in the dining car. Hah! Not only was there no dining car, there was not even a snack machine. So for two and a half days, we ate only the few oranges I had brought. Finally, as the train entered Turkey, a dining car was attached. Audrey and I sat down at a table and had a real meal for the first time in two and a half days. Probably considered unremarkable by some, this meal to us rivaled any prepared by the world's most renowned chefs.

After such a trip, our eventual arrival in Istanbul was rather anticlimactic. It was winter, and the city was covered with snow blackened by soot. Still we did the usual touristy things: we saw the Blue

Mosque and the Bosporus. We spent a lot of time in the *souk*, marveling at the many shops offering gold and carpets. Both Audrey and I ordered gold necklaces with our names inscribed in Arabic. As usual, our friend Sadie, who had flown to Istanbul some days earlier, bought several carpets. Istanbul, with all its marvels, couldn't erase the memories of that train ride. As a final outrage, Montezuma's revenge caught up with me at Sadie's hotel.

Back in Germany

Dresden: Scene of Potential Danger

Not all encounters were amusing or at least non-threatening. One in particular could have been disastrous for me. Soon after the end of communist control in the East, some of the youth began to practice atrocities on those they deemed unfit. Some had come out of their Soviet-imposed hibernation with the same attitudes that were prevalent during the Nazi era half a century earlier: among them, prejudice toward the handicapped, Jews, elderly, and foreigners, especially Turks and Africans. In fact, in 1992 a fire bombing of a home in Mölln killed three members of a Turkish family who had lived in Germany fifteen years. Although two had been born in Germany and were German citizens, they were considered foreigners and, as such, undesirables. In 1993, five members of a Turkish family who had lived for many years in Solligen were targeted. As the family slept one night, a group of youths firebombed the home, killing the middle-aged woman and four others. The reaction of some of the neighboring German women was distressing. One woman being interviewed dismissed the incident as a boyish prank. Other observers cheered. There were also reports of attacks on the elderly. Eventually, though, I felt that travel to the East was safe enough.

In 1994, five years after the opening of East Europe to the West, I took an overnight train to Dresden in former East Germany. The train arrived early in the morning, and, looking for the station's café, I started up some stairs past unopened shops inside the station. As I headed to the 3rd floor, I realized that I was in increasingly deserted areas and that two East German youths were following me. When I heard one of them say, "*Jetzt geht es los*" ("now it begins"), I knew they meant to harm me. I stopped suddenly, turned to them, and said in High German: "Good morning! Could you tell me where the café is?" They were completely surprised. I imagine that they had not seen many lone black females, and to encounter one who spoke *Hoch Deutsch* stunned them so much that, forgetting their original intentions, they answered my question. I thanked them warmly and quickly descended the stairs and hurried into the café, which was full of diners. Soon the two youths entered, sat down, and ordered nothing. As I ate breakfast and read a newspaper, the two got up, went to the door, and paused briefly. Looking in my direction, one announced to the room at large: "The *sau* ('slut') is reading a news-paper." Of course, I didn't react visibly to the insult, the basest one Germans have for a female. Nor did anyone else. I continued to eat and read and thank God for the inner voice that had alerted me to danger. In spite of that bit of ugliness, I enjoyed the rest of my brief stay in Dresden.

Automobile Travel

Although most of my long distance travel in Europe was by train, plane, and ship, on a couple of occasions I braved car travel on European highways to relatively nearby countries like Belgium and France. My reason for preferring to avoid highway travel was that the size of my car made it difficult to find suitable parking and to maneuver small country roads.

In a packet given to the newly recruited African American teach-ers was the advice to avoid taking big American cars to Europe. Well, that particular bit of advice came too late for me: a year before being accepted into the program, I had bought a luxurious Thunderbird equipped with leather seats, power brakes, power steering, and power windows. (I had asked a young church leader for suggestions. He recommended a Thunderbird and helped me to pick out this car—a car suitable for a man but unnecessarily powerful for a woman school teacher.) Yet it was the most beautiful and most expensive car I had ever owned, so there was no way that I was going to give it up. I took it to Germany, where nobody in the whole country had such a big car. Once as I was lying down in the car while waiting for a friend, two German men passed by. One of them observed, "That's not an automobile: that's a steamship."

The car's large size, however, wasn't the main deterrent to my long-distance driving: it was its tremendous power.

A group of friends and I had decided on a drive to Switzerland—a foolhardy venture. Although the group included two males experienced in European driving, no one thought about the fact that we would be driving through the Alps in a car that was not made to navigate narrow, winding roads. So there we were high in the Alps in an S-curve—when the brakes gave out. The slow mountain driving had caused the power brakes to shut down so much so that they couldn't stop the car. At this point I couldn't afford the luxury of panicking: our lives depended on my being able to control a "brakeless" car heading down a mountain. Thank God for the presence of mind to bump repeatedly and gently into the snow-covered sides of the mountain until the car stopped near a path leading to a little town. Understandably shaken, we decided to go into the town's coffee house to recuperate from our ordeal while the car cooled down. After we had calmed down somewhat, we reluctantly returned to the car. Though we didn't relish the thought of getting back into it, we had no choice: without it we would be stranded in a small Alpine town. In addition, I couldn't feasibly abandon the car, especially so far from home. In testing the brakes before driving off, I found that they were again working. So we safely continued our trip.

One evening during this trip, we stopped in a festival hall of a little town. My reception there was overwhelming. People came running up to us. In their eagerness to meet me, they separated me from my friends. Not being prepared for such, I momentarily felt a bit of alarm, but then Uli rescued me from the friendly, not threatening, crowd. They made way for us at tables. One woman told us that she was going on vacation somewhere south and, rubbing my cheeks, said that she would become as brown as I. Honestly, I don't think they had ever before seen in person anybody resembling me.

CHAPTER III

Studying in Germany:
Learning the Language

Some of my German studies took place in American facilities, including a branch of the University of Maryland. Some were very basic non-credit conversational courses prepared by the military for the troops. In my first year I joined such a class. That proved unsatisfying and unsuccessful because the soldiers didn't have the same purpose or commitment to learning German as I had. Most of them were in Germany for a limited time only. Some wanted to learn only enough German to enable them to romance a Fraülein or to order beer in a German club. Some were in the class to earn some military bonus points.   Therefore, their interest in the class appeared to be superficial, unlike mine, which was to learn the language well enough to move about comfortably in the German culture. Their attendance was sporadic, sometimes unavoidably so. They were, after all, in the military and the class was not their priority. Often they were on maneuvers and couldn't attend.   Still, the frequent absences meant that lessons were often repeated, and we made little progress.

After a few weeks I realized that that was not the class for me, so I attended a non-credit summer course (*Ferien Kurse für Ausländer*) at the University of Frankfurt. Because of the short time there, I learned some German but not much. The following fall semester, I enrolled in the Frankfurt branch of the University of Maryland. I enjoyed those courses very much. I'm sorry to admit that my enthusiasm caused me to be quite annoying to some of my classmates. I was so happy to be learning the language that I guess I seemed on the verge of exploding. (When I am interested in something, I sometimes go overboard.)

Anyway, studying as an adult is marvelous. In some of the advanced German classes, the professors and the atmosphere were very informal yet informative. Sometimes there were weekend classes at an out-of-town *Gasthaus* (a small family-run hotel/restaurant), where we sat around tables as we discussed, snacked, and drank wine, beer, sodas, and coffee. I was doing quite well with the structure of the language and the vocabulary, but I couldn't **speak** the language. Everyone in the classes was American, so speaking German always felt so artificial and pretentious that I couldn't do it. The next step, then, was to put myself in an environment where I would be forced to speak the language: the downtown *Inlingua* language school was the perfect place for me. Since there were people from all over the world, our lingua franca was German. If we wanted to communicate, we would have to use German. Soon, speaking in German felt completely natural.

Finally, I was ready to move about in German circles. Not without risk, however: I hadn't mastered those "strange" German verbs. One little vowel could impede one's social success. For example, after an opera performance one evening, my friend Uli and I visited some of his friends. To show that I could carry my part of the conversation, I said: "Yes, an especially exciting part was the scene where the man *hat geschissen*." Well, there were gasps and then silence. Later Uli took me aside and said, "You meant *geschossen*" (shot), "not *geschissen*" (shat).

Of course, verbs weren't the only language problem facing the foreigner: there was the recurrence of one particular street sign. Noticing that the word *Einbahnstrasse* appeared on many signs, my friend Evelyn observed, "There are a lot of streets with that name." She hadn't realized that *Einbahnstrasse* was not a name but a direction: one-way street. Then there was another friend who returned German partings with "I be the same," which she thought the Germans were saying with "*Auf Wiedersehn.*" There was another friend who, having learned no German, offered her own rendition. When speaking with Germans, she adopted some sort of specious accent purporting to be German: "I say to de people vut are you goink to do ahftuh de show?"

CHAPTER IV

Studying in Germany:
Two Life-changing Remarks

I had looked forward to a college education as a way out of the squalor and misery of Suzette Bottom, a world of shacks, kerosene heat, and back-porch toilets—a world in which I had existed for four years. College represented a world of enlightenment among people who read books, whose third person singular verbs ended in sibilants, and who spoke in refined tones, unlike the people of Suzette Bottom, who usually spent Sunday afternoons tossing their recently emptied beer bottles into our front yard and bandying obscenities under our windows. I would find in college my milieu.

So, on the first day of class, I sat in Art Appreciation 101, trying earnestly to express mental acuity, eagerness, and a savoir-faire I most definitely did **not** possess. Then the instructor, a bronze Adonis, walked in. RM epitomized the intellectual of my fantasies—suave, articulate, expressive. I had to have him—his attention and admiration—that is. I had to show him that, though a mere freshman, I ranked among those who possessed esoteric information about the lives of the great. Therefore, in the midst of one of his lectures, I made the first of the two remarks that sent my life on its present course. "Is it true," I asked, "that most of the great artists were funny (gay)?"

Oh, God, why did I ask that particular question? I had never really thought about it, didn't care to know the answer, and wouldn't have known the implications of the answer. Although I had book learning and an extensive vocabulary, my knowledge about the ways of the world came vicariously from books and from friends whose ignorance rivaled my own. Thus, I didn't realize then that I had said something wrong. But, when movement and audible breathing in the classroom ceased, I vaguely sensed something amiss.

Emerging from a well of outrage, the instructor came back with a counterattack. Eyebrows turning somersaults, sensual lips becoming a jagged line, and words issuing needles of ice, he replied: "Young lady, the word is 'homosexual,' not 'funny.' What an artist or anybody else does in his bedroom is his own business."

Ever innocent to the point of naiveté and free from malicious intent, I didn't realize that he was telling me off. I didn't realize that I had directed my question to an avowed homosexual. Only after class did I realize the enormity of my error. Older, more sophisticated male students told me.

Ah, what remorse I suffered for my innocent remark! That the object of my adoration should think me capable of stupid malice proved more than I could bear. From that moment on, I tried to show him my great admiration, my appreciation of the arts, and my intense desire to learn. In the weeks that followed, I sometimes stayed after class and, mutely adoring him, worked on my project in another room. One day I heard him make a disparaging remark about me. Unaware of my presence, he referred to me as "the flat-chested one." I responded as I usually did (and still do) to hurt: I pretended I hadn't heard.

Because he realized the possibility of my having overheard him, his remorse elicited from him extra kindness and consideration to me. Having noticed my interest in and almost total ignorance of classical music, he gave me my first recording—a 45 rpm of famous dramatic sopranos singing arias from popular operas: "Vissi d'arte" from *Tosca* and "Or sai chi l'onore" from *Don Giovanni* among them. Often we talked about opera, and he encouraged me to study voice. He also encouraged my desire to see operas performed in the lands of their origin.

Since that time I have tried to immerse myself in the world of beauty that he revealed to me. I have tried to use the principles he taught in Art Appreciation 101 to create beauty in my surroundings. I did study voice and do sing. Finally, I was living in Europe, where I attended many operas performed in the lands of their origin. I sang duets at the *Nicolai Kirche* in Frankfurt and at Central and Atterbury Chapels. I sang on opera stages with the German American Choir. And I served as one of the soloists of *Zweite Kirche, Christliche Wissenschaft* in Frankfurt, Germany.

Thus, two initially damaging remarks provided the inspiration to raise my life to a level of beauty unimaginable in my earlier years.

An essay submitted to Mr. Schaff
Germany, 24 February 1991

CHAPTER V

Studying in Germany:
From Adversity to Assimilation

Autobiographical Reflections on Excerpts from Zora Neale Hurston's *Invented Lives*

"I come from a long line of domestics," my friend Evelyn says, tongue-in-cheek, when complimented on her immaculate, well-appointed home. This statement is a reference to the fact that her mother, her mother's mother, her aunts—most of the adult females in her family—had at one time or another earned their living as domestics for well-to-do whites. Just as an educated Helga Crane was forced to seek work in Chicago as a domestic, so were many African American women in the first half of the twentieth century.

My own mother, her four sisters, and one brother grew up in relative prosperity on a large farm in Phillip, Mississippi. Her father, a prototype of the self-made man, taught himself to read and eventually became a leader in the African Methodist Episcopal Church and a highly respected landowner. Though he had many children, he saw to it that all received a high school education, which was extremely rare for southern Blacks in the early 1900s. A high school diploma carrying then almost the same weight that a college degree does today, my mother was able to teach in a small Mississippi town. Through a lack of the understanding of proper business procedures, my grandfather lost his farm, his home, his self-esteem, and, in his eyes, his manhood. Thus, no longer having a homestead, my mother and her siblings left the protected confines of their former home and went elsewhere to earn a living.

My mother moved to Memphis, where she met and married my father. After a short-lived togetherness, she began to experience what it meant to be a young, unprotected, unappreciated, struggling African American woman in the first half of the twentieth century. Although she was well-educated for the times, the only jobs she could get were menial ones: cleaning house for whites and working as janitress at military installations. (One sister, who had formerly worked as a bookkeeper for a black business in Mississippi, wound up as a janitress in a tuberculosis hospital in Detroit.) In spite of my mother's comparatively high level of education and her native intelligence, like Helga Crane, she was considered—as an African American woman—not suitable for any on-the-job training program and was consigned to the job of "cleaning shithouses," as my beautiful, outspoken mother put it.

Like that of many of my friends, ours was a single-parent household, with my mother working at jobs she seldom discussed at home. Though we lived in a cold-water, shotgun house with a toilet on the enclosed back porch; though our house was heated by space heaters fueled by kerosene that I regularly carried from the store in a five-gallon can in my scrawny, seven-year-old arms; though the rain often leaked into the front room of that house; my mother insisted that we observe these amenities of civilization: education, good language habits, and, above all, cleanliness. Hands had to be washed often; bodies bathed in tin tubs filled with roasting-pan-heated water; and black elbows, knees, and necks scrubbed with Old Dutch cleanser (my mother's favorite brand, probably because of its excessive abrasiveness).

Recent readings about African American women have helped me to become less condemning of my mother's psychological and verbal abuse and to become more understanding of the forces and pressures operating on her as an attractive, educated, yet unappreciated, unsung African American woman struggling alone to bring up three children and criticized by some as being "hancty" (haughty) and by an older sister as "too proud to accept charity."

Such was the way I grew up—as an African American child of an African American woman shoved into the ranks of those who live in substandard housing and exist on below-subsistence-level income. However, imagination—nurtured by school and radio—was my deliverance from this figurative and literal dimness (each of our three rooms was lit by a single, naked bulb suspended from the ceiling by a two-foot cord). In school I read about alternative lifestyles in which each person had her own room with a silk- or lace-covered bed as its focal point. Lifestyles which afforded a huge, apodal bathtub, filled to the brim with hot water and fragrant bath salts and oils. Lifestyles where the family sat down to a linen-covered table, and from porcelain dishes and crystal goblets breakfasted on **two** pieces of bacon, **two** eggs, **two** pieces of golden toast (like in the ads), fruit preserves, and gallons of milk and orange juice. To this day, such a breakfast is one of the luxuries of my life, to be indulged in only on weekends and holidays, when I have the time to savor each morsel. What to many people is little more than an act of providing sustenance to the body is to me a sybaritic rite.

Radio was also an entry into vicarious participation in alternative lifestyles. Every Saturday I listened to *Let's Pretend*, a program of fairy tales, where I met palaces, castles, fairy godmothers, and Prince Charmings. Through radio, a whole world of beauty opened for me, and I identified wholeheartedly with the heroines of the fairy tales. Sometimes I was the unapproachable ice-queen, with cool, snow-white skin and raven tresses. Other times I was the sun–queen, with golden skin and hair the color of sunshine. I was never an African queen because I didn't know such a being had ever existed. And I

33

waited for Prince Charming. (Though I believed in him ardently throughout most of my life, he never showed up. He was always the **frog** in disguise.) Like Phyllis Wheatley, I assimilated the mentality of the white world.

The (Black) Emulate Trap, or the Psychological Assimilation of a Dark-skinned African-American Woman

In 1972 I announced to a circle of friends and to colleagues at a Chicago high school where I taught that I was moving to Europe. One of the questions asked was "What are you running from?" A passage from one of the reading assignments for this class brought to mind this question. About Nella Larson, Washington asks:

> What happens to a writer who is legally black but internally identifies with both blacks and whites, who is supposed to be content as a member of the black elite but feels suffocated by its narrowness, who is emotionally rooted in the black experience and yet wants to live in the whole world, not confined to a few square blocks and the mentality that make up Sugar Hill?

Though the question above refers to mulattas of the 1920s and 1930s, with a few changes in the text, it could refer to today's professional African American woman.

> What happens to an [educated woman] who is [obviously] black but [being a product of American schools and America's value system] internally identifies with both blacks and whites, who is supposed to be content as a member of the black [professional class] but feels suffocated by its narrowness, who is emotionally rooted in the black experience and yet wants to live in the whole world, not confined to a few square blocks and the mentality that make up Sugar Hill [Parkway, Pill Hill, or any other enclave of black middle-class snobbery]?

34

Though Larsen's major women characters "as black women of the 1920s are marginal to both black and white worlds" in that they are fair enough to "pass," I too have been marginal to both worlds. While there can never be a question of my racial identity, I have been maligned for having "white" interests: the opera and other classical music, British literature, European languages, ocean voyages. Thus, one could say that I'm "passing" in a cultural sense. In fact, some African Americans refer to people like me as Oreo cookies, black on the outside but white on the inside.

Of course, such an assessment is false. I have not abnegated my own culture. Because I have been well educated in American values and mores, I have inculcated—like any apt student—those tastes, interests, and attitudes that were taught to me as part of an American education. Like many other intelligent, educated persons, I want to experience as much as I can of what is good in many cultures, not just the black. I want to enjoy the aurora borealis, the mountain lakes, the fjords of Scandinavia, as well as the gold mines of Ghana and the sculptures of Abu Simbel. I want to appreciate and enjoy Greek and Roman culture as well as that of Timbuktu.

What happens to such people described in the passage quoted from Washington? Some of them go to other countries. Three decades ago I went to Europe, where I could go to the opera without being considered a pretentious traitor to my race and where I could study Italian at an Italian university without being made to feel that I should be studying Swahili.

Larsen's "...spiritual vacuity" of the black bourgeoisie still exists in the second half of the century, especially among some men. Several years ago, when I mentioned at a club meeting that I wanted to get home early enough to watch *Madame Butterfly* on television, some of the people present exchanged slightly disdainful looks. Another time, an African American male visited my home (not at my invitation) and noticed my many books and classical records. Infuriated, he launched a diatribe against "phony people who act white." On one visit to the States, I met with a male friend who soon began his favorite topic, the denunciation of all whites. When I refused to join in and, I guess, displayed a bit of boredom, he half-jokingly said, "Go back to Europe, where you belong." Like Marita Bonner, I know personally "the sense of being trapped in the narrow and stultifying world of the black bourgeoisie."

Ambivalent Attitudes toward African American Men

African American men and I have decided to part company forever and to cease the pretense that we can enter into a meaningful relationship. I have finally discovered that men of my generation have suffered irreparable damage from having grown up in the crippling years before the "black power cultural revolution," when African Americans began to find their own identity and to exult in their heritage. I have seldom been successful in establishing a meaningful relationship with an African American man. Having been damaged myself in my formulative years by hearing them referred to as "dogs" by some of my female relatives and having heard African American men refer to the women as "castrating Sapphires with overly big behinds," I must ruefully confess that I am no longer willing to expend energy on a seemingly "impossible dream."

To be fair to them, however, I must say that I believe *The Color Purple's* portrayal of the sexual abuse of a stepchild and the subsequent wrenching away from her the children born of that incestuous rape to be an anomaly among African American men. Nor have I ever known any to be as physically or as emotionally brutal as Mister. (I do admit, however, that I had an uncle who used to "discipline" his young wife with a belt—until she broke a pitcher over his head the last time he tried it.)

Many of the African American men that I knew or knew of were simply absent (like my father) or rejecting (also like my father). Conversations with other African American women and my own experiences reveal that too many of the men view women, not as persons whose well-being matters in the least, but as objects upon which to bestow the largess of the male's sexual prowess. Too many use women to validate their manhood, taking pride in the number of women who "swell the rout" of those who succumb to the irresistible marvels of their phalluses and thus confirm the men's belief in their superior sexual potency, the majority of them having little political or economic potency. I will, however, always be grateful to African American men, for one of them was the indirect cause of my moving to Europe, which I love. But that is a chapter for another time.

Addendum to "From Adversity to Assimilation": July 2008

In the above depiction of African American men, I have been unfair to many. Certainly not all are so shallow and promiscuous as to measure their worth solely by their anatomy. There are those who rank among the finest men in the universe. They are avatars of manliness: they are dependable, caring, responsible, intelligent, mature, strong, and truly sexy. In spite of the inequality of opportunity and the low status society has handed them, some have risen above the negative images assigned to them in movies, newspapers, and police reports. I would be totally remiss as an African American woman if I failed to recognize the nobility and strength of men who have risen to heights in spite of the heavy heel seeking to tread them into the dust. It takes a strong man to rise from the dust with a thousand-pound weight of racial discrimination on his neck. Such men include my maternal grandfather James Cummings; my brother Gerald Wells; my nephew DeAndre Wells; my cousin Patricia's husband Errol Thomas; my cousin Patricia's son Mabon; my "adopted" nephews Cory and Kyle Whitaker and Robert and Paul Jude; my friend Evelyn's husband Bob Jude; my friend Sageta's husband Rudy Jackson; my friend Debbie's husband Charles Raikes; my cousin Richard Townsel, and a college friend Robert Mairley. As Mark Anthony says: "So are they all, all honorable men." That I had unpleasant contacts was due to my own failure to discern the silver plate from the sterling.

An essay submitted to Dr. Tobe Levin
Frankfurt, Germany, 20 June 1992

CHAPTER VI

Studying in Germany: Toni Morrison and the Literature of the Grotesque: *Sula*

The following excerpt from the *Library Journal's* critical review of Tony Morrison's novel *Sula* shows incredible ignorance and offensiveness in its assigning aberrant behavior to a whole group of people.

> "This is…an evocation of a whole black community during a span of 40 years…the recreation of the black experience in America with both artistry and authenticity."

Artistry, yes: authenticity, no.

Newsweek calls it "exemplary **fable**" (emphasis mine) and the *Los Angeles Free Press* refers to it as "truly quality **fiction**." (Again emphasis mine.) For that's exactly what *Sula* is, fiction whose characters are so divorced from real life that they are grotesque beings who, like other fabulous beings, speak and act (in part) like humans but really aren't. They are not "recreations of the black experience"; rather, they are complete creations of a fiction writer's mind.

I have never met or heard of any black Americans who exhibit the behavior of the caricatures who people Morrison's novel. It is disturbing that educated members of respected media, who ought to be familiar with various ethnic groups living in their midst, would be so ill-informed as to lump millions of a race under some nebulous blanket as the "black experience." It is alarming also to think that these people are so unfamiliar with black Americans that they could perceive those distortions presented in *Sula* to be "authentic representations" of even its most bizarre creatures. They certainly do not represent me or any of the myriad people I have encountered in my many decades of life.

Morrison's characters are so grotesque that they are degenerates—complete to the etymological sense of the word in their being "away from the race" of humans as far as normal behavior is concerned.

The character Eva's deliberately cutting off her leg for whatever reason is simply too absurd to be credible. If Morrison intends it to be an act of maternal love which enabled Eva to feed her starving family, I find it implausible. The novel says about Eva, "Under Eva's distant eyes, her own children grew up stealthily." This passage reveals a lack of parental concern and guidance. Yet we should believe that she loved her son Plum so much that she killed him to end the ravages of his drug addiction. Eva says, "I just thought of a way he could die, not all scrunched up inside my womb [where he would suffocate], but like a man." So to save him from him from suffocating, she douses him with kerosene and sets him on fire. How totally absurd, how ridiculously illogical that, to save a child from the inferno of drug addiction, a mother would turn him into a human conflagration!

Sula, Eva's granddaughter, is even more grotesque than her grandmother. First, there's that business of cutting off part of her finger in an attempt to protect herself and Nel from the gang of white boys who harass them on the way to Nel's house. "Sula raised her eyes to them. Her voice was quiet. 'If I can do that to myself, what do you suppose I'll do to you?'" And so, in mutilating herself, she "protects" both herself and Nel from an attack by the white boys, who escape unscathed while Sula stands there dripping blood. Morrison has Sula herself refer to the incident as "bizarre."

Sula's reaction to her accidental killing of the little boy is not one of remorse and anguish for the boy, but one of terror of discovery. "Had he [Shadrach] seen?" (63). Also the following passage shows her lack of remorse: "...her one major feeling of responsibility had been exorcised on the bank of a river with a closed place in the middle." (This refers to Chicken Little's drowning.) How absolutely grotesque and inhuman!

Another act that shows Sula's grotesqueness is her thoughtless destruction of the marriage of a friend who had been so close that they were "two throats with one eye" (147). When trying to find some reason for Sula's affair with her husband, Nel asks why. Sula replies: "Jude filled up the space; that's all." She offers as reason nothing as acceptable, understandable, or admirable as all-consuming love.

As horrifying as these three examples are, the most grotesque incident of all, the one that truly shows Sula's degeneracy—her being outside the realm of human behavior—is her reaction to her mother's burning alive. After the funeral, the grandmother Eva recalls that Sula had just watched her mother burn, that she had stood immobile, not trying to help her. "Eva...remained convinced that Sula had watched Hannah burn, not because she was paralyzed [from shock], but because she was interested" (178). Sula herself later says of the incident: "I stood there watching her burn and was thrilled. I wanted her to keep on jerking, to keep on dancing." Not even the lowest animal would stand idly by, relishing its mother's horrible agony.

Morrison says, "...the Peace women loved all men." Hannah's carryings-on with the husbands of her friends can scarcely be called "love-making." For by its very nature erotic love is selective. Yet Morrison says Hannah would [copulate] with practically anything, anywhere. To label this behavior the mindless acts of animals is to be overly generous, for animals rut only during estrus.

Of Sula, Morrison says, "He (Ajax) dragged her under him and made love to her." Neither Sula nor Ajax knows the meaning of love. (Morrison says also that Ajax loved his mother, but I doubt it.) Loves includes a caring for and a conscious attempt to effect the well-being of the loved one. Yet Sula often has difficulty in remembering the name of a partner even in the midst of their sexual activities. "When her partner disengaged himself, she looked up at him in wonder trying to recall his name" (123). How could Sula love someone who was so insignificant to her? Thus, "love" as a term for the animal-like act in which Sula and Ajax engaged is a misnomer. A more accurate depiction would be "the mechanical coupling of two sex-driven machines." Another fact that shows further Sula's degenerate nature is that she is aroused by a man whose only claim to distinctiveness is his "magnificently foul mouth." Also grotesque is the imagery she uses to express her desire to know him completely. She says that she wants to "rub real hard on his bone" and "scrape away at the gold" and "tap away at the alabaster." I'm not quite sure what Morrison means with this passage, but the harsh connotations of the words "rub," "scrape," and "tap" convince me that the meaning is not good.

Nel, who seemed to be one of the few normal characters, turns out to be grotesque also. Toward the end of the book, she admits that her calm behavior at the drowning of Chicken Little resulted, not from "maturity, serenity, and compassion, but from… enjoyment in seeing him die." She says. "Why didn't I feel bad when it happened? How come it felt so good to see him fall?"

Such grotesque characters above are not representatives of the African American community. It is true that in some parts of this novel Morrison does portray some of the harsh realities of African American women in America, yet it is inaccurate and degrading to say that Sula and Nel "combine to create an unforgettable rendering of what it means and costs to exist and survive as a black woman in America!" Where in the African American community

41

are there such aberrations as the Peace women? Contrary to being "recreations of the black experience in America," Morrison's novel ranks right up there with those of other writers of the horror genre.

Paper submitted for the class Black Women Writers
June 1992

CHAPTER VII

Studying in Germany: A Fledgling Diva

D uring my junior year in College, I felt the time had come to introduce to the world its newest operatic phenomenon, me. A vocal competition for which I considered myself extremely qualified had been announced. Hadn't my singing talent been demonstrated time and time again? Couldn't I sing louder than many of my neighbors in the college choir? Hadn't I been given a solo line or two for Wednesday morning chapel services? And, as for the ability necessary to sing in Italian, I was already a recognized linguist. While it was true that I had never studied Italian, I had had a whole semester of high school Latin. Wasn't it true that Latin was the mother of Italian, the language of many operas? My ability to sing in French, another opera-related language, was uncontested. Everyone in our small student body could attest to my fluency in French, revealed through my having spoken these words in a scene from *Le Cid*: "Seeya. Seeya. Juice-tees. Rodriguez ay tooyay mon pairuh!" This was a southern rendition of *"Sire! Sire! Justice! Rodriguez a tué mon pere!"* Yes, I was a linguist *par excellence,* so Italian would present no problem to me. I would teach myself an aria from an Italian opera.

Thus armed with sophomoric confidence that I was to be the next African American *prima donna assoluta,* I signed up for the competition.

A week before the competition, I began assiduous study of the aria "Ah, fors' è lui" from the opera *La Traviata.* That only a week remained before the competition was no cause of concern to a person of my intelligence. I had already demonstrated my intellectual acumen. I was greatly admired by freshmen for lowering my thick glasses, forming my eyebrows into questions, and succinctly murmuring, "How existential!" "What is the relevance of that statement?" "That hardly seems feasible." "Wow! That's deep."

With the realization of this ability to sustain me, I prepared to enter the world of the truly great, to be heralded as another Leontyne Price. Though I had had no coaching sessions from the music department and had used only recordings to learn the pronunciation of the lyrics, I felt ready to set the opera world ablaze with the virginal purity and intense power of my golden soprano.

Wearing a pink, fourteen-dollar strapless gown held on my one-hundred-five-pound frame by pieces of tape and fifty safety pins, I swept smiling onto the stage à la Loretta Young and looked into the audience. Hundreds of eyes were fixed on my mouth as the audience waited expectantly and respectfully to hear the new marvel. My confident smile locked into a grimace of stage fright. As the accompanist played the introduction, I tried to position my mouth, my lips, my diaphragm to make that first sound. Nothing moved. Then teeth clenched, jaws locked, lips became lead, and breathing came sporadically.

Again the accompanist played the signaling portion. This time every part of me went into motion: lips flapped furiously together; knees performed a rare kind of hula, involving no movement of feet; arms and hands did a Balinese dance; and head punctuated the rhythms of the piano. Still no sound from *la prima donna assoluta.*

When it became clear to me that no sound *would* emerge from my throat on that occasion, my thought was no longer of being acclaimed voice of the decade. It was one of simple survival: how to get off that stage and still retain some bit of dignity. To do so, I had to make it clear that the whole matter was simply beyond my human powers. I had two choices: I could die or I could "get sick." I chose the latter: positioning myself theatrically, I fainted. Thus, I was carried off the stage with my dignity intact. After all, I couldn't help it if I got sick, could I?

An essay submitted to Dr. Jeffrey N. Golub
8-12 August 1994

CHAPTER VIII

Studying in England

As the taxi neared our destination, I could see the shadows of a huge estate, cast by the full moon. At the end of the hedge-lined driveway sat Wroxton Abbey, serene and majestic. Tired, hungry, and almost despairing of ever finding the place, I watched with gratitude as the taxi approached the entrance of the magnificent manor house, where stood Prince Charming in the guise of a mere mortal.

Because I was exhausted from having traveled a day and a half from Frankfurt to reach the Fairleigh Dickinson's European campus in the tiny village of Wroxton, England, near Banbury, I would probably have found attractive anyone who opened the door to the abbey, which was to be my academic haven for the next two months. Yet he was truly an attractive man as he stood framed by the warm lights of the Great Hall of the mansion. He wore a tweed jacket, tan corduroy trousers, and a smile that cut through my fatigue and hunger and wrapped itself around my heart. With that attire and the pipe that hung from his mouth, he was a picture of the Cambridge academician. Since he offered to take my luggage to my room upstairs, I assumed him to be one of the general handy men on the campus.

However, the next day as we students got acquainted in the buttery, I learned that he was Doctor X, one of the tutors (professors) at the university.

During idyllic weeks spent attending lectures in the regal former house of a British aristocrat, strolling around the vast grounds of fruit trees and lily ponds, studying by rose bushes, lolling on the lawn, and eating at the refectory tables in the dining hall, I saw Him. Always I saw Him. He was reserved and seemed aloof. Yet I thought I sometimes saw a gleam in his eyes when he looked at me—and look at me he did. Sometimes I would look across the dining hall to where he sat at the off-limits-to-students table and see him looking at me.

Cupid's arrows are so potent that they reduced me, a fully grown, professional woman, to a simpering, giggling state of juvenility. I became absolutely giddy, shy, and fatuous. If I chanced to look at him directly, I would blush and quickly avert my eyes. Yet my leisure hours were spent in devising ways to run into him—accidentally. I figured out his routine. After dinner, he and another professor would stroll over to a nearby pub that was off limits to us, the students. (Though most of the summer students were professional adults, we had to abide by the rules for the undergrads, who attended the winter sessions.) After a couple of hours at the pub, he would return to the campus. Sometimes he went to his office. Sometimes he went jogging. On rare occasions he went downstairs to the TV room. (I never had the courage to go there when I knew he'd be there. After all, I had no desire to appear gauche; I wanted our encounters to seem to be chance.) So I would stalk him from a safe distance until I would "accidentally" run into him.

Then one day it happened. Fate contrived to set the stage for one of the most romantic interludes of my life. The special evening began with a cocktail party on the lawn of the dean's house. For the first time since my arrival at the estate weeks before, we talked together. He spent the entire time with me. Of course, my whole being became one radiant smile. After the cocktail time, we walked across

47

the grounds to the dining hall. While we waited in the buttery to be called to dinner, he and I talked. We were both reluctant to go in to dinner, for we knew that custom dictated that he sit at the head table with the other faculty and I with the students. Yet in that candle-lit room I was aware of him as we sat across the room from each other. After dinner we all returned to the buttery for conversation and drinks. There he and I talked, gazed into each other's eyes, and, completely oblivious to those around us, kissed, and went to his room.

Unfortunately, my dream was soon shattered. In the midst of passionate kisses, he told me something I had heard rumored for weeks: he was engaged to be married in a month and a half. God, those words actually rent my heart. Married! In a month and a half! I unwound myself from the embrace and went to my room. The brief flame had ended badly.

The next day, after having confided in a friend, I ran into him on campus and she kind of laughed. I saw him draw into himself. I think he felt that I had been teasing him. For the next few days, we avoided each other. One evening it was impossible to do so, and we were once again in the buttery. When I went to the counter to order a drink, I had to pass him. My hands shook so violently that I had to use **both** hands to hold one little glass. (Of course, the whole room was aware of some kind of drama, for they had seen the kiss and the exit together.) When I smiled and spoke, he answered me very coldly. In response to a note I placed in his mailbox, he sent a cryptic one saying that his fiancée would arrive on campus within a couple of days. I was totally devastated. I returned to my room and wept silently until all tears were spent (but only for the time being).

On the day of the farewell cookout, I went to the home of a DoDDS teacher who lived in a nearby village. During the two days I spent there, I tried to keep my unhappiness hidden from her. But no. She was aware of my pain. I don't understand it: I don't know why I was so affected. To this day, I still feel the pain whenever I think of that time. I never saw him after that. The summer session ended a couple of days later, and I went back to Germany, where for many weeks I was a zombie teaching students who had no idea that their teacher was grieving over a lost dream.

Despite my heartache, study in England was rewarding in ways I could never have foreseen. I saw my first live Shakespearean drama, one performed by the Royal Shakespeare Company, including the pre-movie star Judi Dench. Also, I had my introduction to high tea, which I had assumed to be the same as afternoon tea, only served a bit later than the usual times. One day, when we were scheduled to attend a modern presentation of *Hamlet* in Stratford on Avon, we were told that the evening meal would be a 5-pm high tea. Not having a taste for tea and sandwiches just then, I stayed in my room until time to leave for the theater. Great was my chagrin when I discovered that I had missed a meal that included steak, vegetables, salad, etc. High tea has nothing to do with tea but with the hour. It is usually served at 6 pm and is what we refer to as dinner or supper.

Traditionally, English cuisine is bland, but the meals at Wroxton Abbey were always good. The college never skimped on the quality or quantity of its meals. The breakfast was especially delicious: Canadian bacon, ropes of sausages with strange names, ham sizzling in its own juice, eggs accompanied by a grilled tomato, English muffins, jams, potatoes, and plenty of hot tea and coffee. This meal was not to be missed. Other pleasantries included visits and lectures by noted authors and critics, who gave erudite lectures that usually went over our heads. (One lecturer would pause ever so often and ask: "You don't know that?") Once on a field trip with the class, I received a lovely compliment from an older Englishman, who said in the presence of many of my college mates: "Excuse me, Mum, but you're a fine-looking woman." (Is it any wonder that I stayed in Europe for twenty-three years?) I've always liked to learn, but learning in such surroundings was like being in Eden.

CHAPTER IX

Studying in Italy: Perugia

One year I decided to study Italian in Italy. Through a friend, I found that San Francisco State University offered study abroad courses during the summers. After completing arrangements, I left my DoDDS sophomores behind and, assuming their role as student, headed to Italy, where I would spend the first of my two July sessions studying at *L'Università per Stranieri á Perugia*.

On the train I met a young Italian who was returning from Germany, where he had gone to meet someone with whom he had been communicating via post. He revealed that the meeting was very disappointing because he had found the man to be quite unattractive. By the end of the train trip, Stefano had given me his phone number and his address, which was near the place where I would be lodging. Some days later, after settling in at the university, I visited Stefano, his mother, his sister, and his brother. From the very beginning, I felt totally welcomed by the family. The mother prepared delicious meals and drove me around the neighboring villages. I felt so comfortable that I even took a couple of American students to meet the family. Stefano was very friendly but inexplicably announced to all that he was gay. I never understood his need to reveal his sexuality when to do so was irrelevant to the situation. I didn't wonder why the family extended such ready acceptance of me, someone they hardly knew. I assumed that it was due to my affability and natural charm.

But the next summer I found out the real reason. By then, I was able to communicate—though just barely—in Italian. One day the mother exclaimed jubilantly: "I'm going to be a mother-in-law!" Since I had returned after a year, she assumed that Stefano and I had a relationship. Having discovered what she thought was an affair unsuitable for a young Italian, my landlady, who had my passport, called the mother to let her know that I was too old for Stefano. What Signora C. didn't know was that the mother had so despaired of her son's ever having a heterosexual relationship that she would have accepted anything, so long as it was female. In spite of the fact that that I was an African American a couple of decades older than her son and almost twice his height, she was ecstatic over the prospect of his finally getting married.

But Stefano soon and most decidedly rid her of that delusion. One day while I was visiting, a young Italian came by and, confessing to Stefano that he had heard of his sexual prowess, disappeared into the bedroom with him for a protracted length of time. The mother was absolutely devastated. I felt so sorry for her that I couldn't visit anymore after that. The family had been humiliated in front of me, a visitor.

Studying abroad for me is the best way to study. It removes the tedium of study and replaces it with an activity that benefits both mind and body. Not only does the student learn about the country and the people, she actually meets the people and interacts with them in their culture. She gets to hear them speaking their language while interacting with one another. She notes the nuances of the language and sees the accompanying gestures. This total immersion makes learning a language a normal occurrence instead of a must-do assignment.

At the university, all courses were taught by Italian professors, who spoke with us in Italian only. Doing so was both practical and effective. There were students from all over the world and with various levels of proficiency in Italian. Some were teachers of Italian in their own countries, some were young people from junior year study-abroad programs at their universities, some were nuns with their own agenda, and some were people who simply loved the sounds of foreign languages. For me, study in Perugia was an idyllic vacation. I was pampered beyond measure. (Of course, I realized that such pampering was not personal but purely economic. But that didn't diminish my enjoyment.) I had my own private room in the home of Signora C., whose son, a doctor, objected to her taking in boarders. At the end of a day of studying and field trips to places like the *Perugina* candy factory, I looked forward to the home-cooked meals awaiting us, Signora C.'s four student residents. I didn't have to launder, clean house, iron, or cook. All I had to do was to enjoy the study experience.

Study abroad benefited the students physically, too, because most had no cars there, so it was necessary to walk everywhere. My section of town was quite a distance from the university's location. Every day, I walked to my morning sessions, back home for lunch, back to school for evening classes, and back home for dinner. Sometimes I walked back to the town center for the students' enjoyable evening pastime of strolling through the center, eating ice cream, and drinking various Italian specialties. I was able to eat as much pasta and ice cream as I wanted—without gaining one unwanted pound. Could study be any better?

My relations to professors are usually positive. They recognize in me traits that make teaching a pleasure—a love of knowledge and an appreciation for the person who imparts it. So it was at the university. However, there was one professor who wasn't interested in me or my love of knowledge. In fact, he didn't know me at all. Our class was held in the *Aula Magna*, a huge lecture hall seating hundreds. His only public recognition of me was a negative one. Because of an incident with him, I learned how my students must feel when I mistakenly accuse them of being inattentive. Since my San Francisco State group had been on a field trip with our American professor the day before, we had missed the Italian professor's important lecture on some very difficult verb tenses. When we attended the next day's class, I took notes during the lecture. Obviously assuming that I was engrossed in something other than his lecture, he called to me from a distance of a football field: "*Signorina*, you are not paying attention." Since my Italian was limited to simple phrases and clauses like "I am very well, thank you," how could I protest? How could I explain that I was trying to catch up on what I had missed while I had been legitimately absent with my American professor (who was in charge of the group)? I couldn't, so I had to remain unjustly chastised.

I later heard that this same professor was making plays for some of the cute young students in the class. Even though the lecture hall was large and held many students, he was able to spot the ones with whom he wanted a dalliance. A couple of the chosen were in our San Francisco group. All too soon, the session ended and I returned to Germany.

However, the following summer came soon enough, and Mary, a colleague, satisfied her years-long desire to study in Perugia. Together we went. Although both of us were professional adults, in Perugia we were as giddy and as carefree as any of the young students we met. Mary and I had so much fun that we sometimes behaved like naughty children. For example, we had a private joke that used to send us into hysterics. In one of our classes, there was a young American southerner whose pronunciation of Italian was so southern and incorrectly accented that it was hilarious. Whenever Mary and I alluded to a mistake of any kind, all we had to do was to repeat his most infamous sentence—pronunciation and all—and we would be overcome with laughter.

Mary was a hit with everybody—the American and foreign students and the Italian professors. In fact, one of the young Italian professors was so enchanted with her that he often invited her to participate in one of the town's evening delights, a walk to the town center to enjoy a *gelato*. My landlady learned of the friendship and spoke with Mary's landlady of the inappropriateness of this relationship between yet another older American and a young Italian male. Again, she had misunderstood: there was no romance involved.

Another beautiful summer vacation had ended, and it was back to Germany to work.

CHAPTER X

Studying in Italy: Rome

Rome: Monday, 22 June 1987

After a very restful fifteen-hour direct train ride from Frankfurt, I arrived at Roma Termini. As soon as I approached the station, a man who purported to be a taxi driver steered me to a waiting car, which had no signs of a taxi about it. I remembered that in our packet of papers from the university was a warning against taking anything other than a bona fide taxi. I had planned to wait a day or two before attempting to speak Italian. But, in the scramble for a taxi, I forgot such niceties as correct syntax and grammar and babbled something that translates roughly as "You taxi? You take me?" Encouraged by success at having made myself understood, I sat back and began a very elementary conversation, limited naturally to the weather. "*Qui a Roma c'è molto sole. A Francoforte, invece, non c'è mai il sole.*"

Arriving at the hotel, I was pleasantly surprised to learn that we were staying at such a classy hotel. Usually I stay at rather ratty ones. One in Spain was so bad that it almost cost me a friend. The worst, though, was in Cairo. Unknowingly, I shared a room with a cat, which came in through a broken place in the door. The day I wanted to kill him was the day I returned to the room to find that he'd left a big pile in the middle of one of the beds. Another problem was that, one night while taking a shower down the hall, I discovered that the window which opened inward was not on the outside of the building but led instead to a passageway inside the seedy hotel. So I imagine that for a couple of days, I had unwittingly been playing Bathsheba to the male hotel staff. Understandably, then, here in Rome I basked in luxury—a shower in my room, a balcony overlooking the patio, and a telephone!

After a refreshing shower and nap, I learned that Martha, a colleague, had arrived. She suggested that we have dinner in the Piazza Navona. She had visited it some years before and was glad to learn that the hotel was located nearby. With Asmik, Martha's roommate, we admired the square, especially the three Bernini fountains and the obelisk, which had been stolen from Egypt, as we learned from Asmik.

Rome: Tuesday, 23 June 1987

This day in class I was so excited by the composition and nature of the class that I had to force myself to exercise some sort of constraint on my joy in being in the class. The realization that I had the opportunity to relate academically and socially with people from a variety of cultures, lands, and experiences in situations where we would learn to treasure even more the value of other cultures and other ways of looking at the world was momentarily almost more than I could contain. These class members (and certainly the professor) were rich—rich with knowledge of other ways of doing things, with other languages, other music, and other standards of beauty. I've always found it desirable to be around people who know—because I want to know. From the wealth of such people as these, I could learn very much. This was what I'd always dreamed of, starting from my early years as I sat, a solitary child under a table, playing with my clothespin people, who spoke some of the many languages I made up.

I experienced from another point of view a situation which impacts on the whole Western world. Asmik is a lovely, gracious woman whose mere presence would grace any city in the world. Yet she had great difficulty in obtaining a visa to participate in this program. After months of delay and numerous documents of proof of her intention to study, she was finally given the necessary clearance to enter Italy. I know that there are reasons for such caution. Yet Asmik's being subjected to hassles simply because she is Arab made me very sad. Maybe such a thing as her having been a part of the class will help to ease the East-West tensions—if only in the most infinitesimal way.

Later that day, Ari, a Brazilian in the class, told me of an apartment that was available at a much lower price than that of the hotel. After much changing of my mind, I called Ari about two in the morning and agreed to share the apartment with him. Funny thing is that, though Ari is Brazilian and I American, I felt a kinship with him. I think it was his personality—so open, so knowledgeable, so gallant—that caused me to feel a kind of connection to him. (I wonder whether his tan color has anything to do with it. Certainly, he didn't feel any connection with **my** color. Brazilians are even more color-conscious than African Americans. In his country, he's considered Caucasian.)

Rome: Wednesday, 24 June 1987

During today's lecture, several statements made specific impressions on me and evoked strong memories, some pleasant and some not so very. One such statement was that in our culture we must constantly be doing something, that to do nothing was considered undesirable and the person unworthy. My mother, evidently also a proponent of such thinking, seemed to have as a major goal in life the determination that I would always be doing something, even if it meant simply running to and from the grocery store to pick up a single item or two or my looking in vain for an object that I had lost but she had found and hidden. That consumed lots of activity!

For the past few years, I've had the conviction that one does actually need time in which she does nothing, in which she can simply be. I'd like to think that I have finally arrived at that point. For example, Saturday is the day when I do almost nothing. But I think down deep inside I still feel that I'm committing a venial (I think that's what the Catholics call it) sin. I think I subconsciously try to justify this day of rest by keeping extremely busy during the rest of the week. I think I announce with pride that my after- work activities include a voice lesson, a church meeting, choir rehearsal until 10 p.m., sometimes an all-day Saturday rehearsal when a concert date is approaching, an Italian lesson, work on the Sunday solo, and the actual singing of the solo on Sunday morning.

While I do keenly enjoy what I do, I'm not so sure that part of the satisfaction doesn't come from being able to say: "See how busy I am."

After I've done enough during the week to justify hours of doing nothing—no housecleaning, no shopping, no visiting—I set aside Saturday and Sunday afternoons to enjoy living. I eat a very late breakfast, read omnivorously from the *Biblical Archeology Review* to *Redbook* to *The World of Islam* to *Alfred Hitchcock's Mystery Magazine*. After a while, I switch on the video to whatever interests me at the moment: a Bolshoi Ballet Company's presentation of the *Nutcracker* or a zany *Pink Panther* comedy or a steamy *Decameron* tale in Italian. All of this I do while lying in bed. So naturally next comes a most marvelous, lazy nap, which I enjoy undisturbed, for I take the phone off the hook. Thus, for a few hours each week, I enjoy the hedonistic pleasure of doing nothing other than enjoying life.

Still another statement relevant to my life evoked pleasant memories. This was the statement that our experiences leave us changed and have some impact on our community. My first luxury liner cruise is evidence of that statement. Years ago, in order to mitigate the aftereffects of a bad relationship, I wanted to do something beautiful and elevating for myself. I decided on a cruise—a very big step for a person who had spent most of her life up to that point between just above the poverty line and, as a teacher in Memphis and Chicago, genteel poverty. That cruise changed my entire life—from my aspirations to my accomplishments. Because of that trip, I saw for the first time in my life foreigners: New Yorkers, Bostonians, Puerto Ricans, Jamaicans, and Italians. When I stepped off the gangplank into the ship itself, an Italian cruise liner, I began the first step of my new life. The luxury of that ship let me see and be a part of gracious living; the gourmet cuisine brought about a lasting interest in exotic foods; hearing Italian reawakened a life-long desire to learn other languages, to experience other cultures, to know other nationalities. And, for the first time in my life, I was accorded all the admiration and attention given to the truly beautiful. (Of course, I later realized that it was more my novelty than any great beauty of mine.) I was absolutely surprised by the attention I got from the Italian crew. In fact, one of the crew was reprimanded for taking me, a passenger, onto the deck for a talk. Thus, for a long time after I returned to earth—my home and my mundane affairs—I was unshakably convinced that I was absolutely irresistible. (However, the guys on my block were doing a darn good job of not only resisting but also ignoring me.) Still, some of them noticed an assuredness about me. The new awareness that I could move successfully among the world's citizens, that people from other cultures found me interesting and desirable, that they would allow me to learn about them—all of this changed my life so wonderfully that I can never cease to be grateful for that experience. As a result of it, I eventually moved to Germany, where for twenty-three years I saw much of the world. This experience certainly had an effect on my community. From that time on, my interest in the ethnicity of my students and of other people around me grew. I renewed my study of Spanish and German and later began Italian.

Rome: Thursday, 25 June 1987

Today the lecture included a discussion of homeostasis. I'm still not sure what it means, but it seems to have something to do with learning through dissonance and a lack of balance. The professor gave this example. If someone moves some item in your home, you can feel it because what you have designed as your homeostasis has been disturbed. What the psychological implications are I don't know. I do know that I find very annoying a person's doing so. I was seeing C., a guy who used to rearrange my furniture whenever he came to visit. If I had one of my big chairs facing the center of the room, within a short time he'd have it facing the window. If I had the table set for dinner in the living room, he'd move the dinner to the kitchen. If I had the lights dimmed and candles providing atmosphere, he'd attack the light switch with a vengeance, flooding the room with light. (I later learned that in his work circle he was known as Mr. Contrary.)

I spent most of this day as I did the day before, in a sedentary—or more correctly said—prone position, much to my distress. For two days I'd had an attack of intense intestinal pains with accompanying hemorrhoids. I had never experienced such pain before. Worse was that the only body waste I could expel was urine. In addition to being sorely incapacitated (I could barely walk to class or sit in the seat in the classroom), I was humiliated. Here was I, a world traveler who had walked the length of Luxor from the temples at Karnak to the boats crossing the Nile over to the Valley of the Kings; who had walked the entire *peripherique* (it seemed) of Paris; who had walked the hills of Perugia several times a day—here was I, felled by something so unspeakable in polite company, so debilitating as hemorrhoids. With envy I listened to my seminar-mates talk of the awe-inspiring monuments they were seeing. Yet my activities were limited to creeping to and from class, reviewing and previewing assignments, and passively practicing Italian through watching television.

The previous two days were days of reflecting. One such reflection was that the Italians pay scant attention to tourists or other foreigners. After years of living in Germany, where my every movement was unabashedly noted; after years of causing near collisions just by walking down German streets or just being in a car on the Autobahn; after causing the strollers during intermission at the opera house to stumble when they saw me standing by having a glass of wine with friends; after having my cheeks rubbed in provincial Swiss towns; after having my presence announced as I stepped from a train in Irun, a Spanish border town; and after being asked on occasions for my autograph; I found blissful the relative anonymity afforded me in this European capital.

Rome: Saturday, 27 June 1987

I'd begun to recuperate. The problem was more serious than I had thought. I think I had a touch of botulism, because it felt as if my intestines were paralyzed. Feeling better, I went on business to the via Margutta. Afterwards, I walked along the piazza di Spagna, admiring the streets between the piazza and the via del Corso. Though I had no intention of buying anything, it was a joy to stroll past the elegant shops of the vias Borgogna and Condotti.

Later I saw the "wedding cake" Asmik had told us about in her briefing—the monument to Vittorio Emanuele II. Some are repulsed by it, saying it is ugly. I can't understand how anyone could fail to be awed by it. To me it is absolutely beautiful. Its gleaming whiteness and classical lines make it quite a noble piece. But what do I know about the merits of architecture? I just know I like it.

Florence: Monday, 29 June 1987

The class and I were in Florence. Again, I was extremely pleased with our attractive hotel. Hoda, Martha, Asmik, Ari, and I sampled Florentine fare at a nearby restaurant that offered food both delicious and sumptuous. Florence is a bustling city even at night. After living for many years in Germany, where the city locks itself up after ten p.m., it was exhilarating to be able to go out at night and find interesting places open with crowds of people milling about. Both the Italians and the Spanish share my practice of having dinner/supper at 8 p.m. or later.

Florence: Tuesday, 30 June 1987

As one guide book says, it would take months to see everything in Florence. In fact, it would take days in the Uffizzi alone. I had planned to devote time there to viewing Donatello and Brunelleschi. I had also planned to revisit Michelangelo's *David*. But, because of an inestimable number of visitors to both the Uffizzi and the Accademia, both places proved to be inaccessible. I had to limit my viewing to the Duomo, the Piazza della Signoria, and the Bargello. I didn't recognize the spot where the prophet Savonarella was burned at stake. I did note again the statue of Neptune that was supposed to have been ruined by Ammannati, but in my ignorance I thought it impressive.

Since the Michelangelo *David* was impossible to reach, I abandoned my plan to see it again in order to compare it with the Donatello. Instead, I decided to look at the Donnatello on its own merits. The Bargello was almost empty. When an English language tour group came in, I stood near and was able to listen for a moment or two before the guide, a little miffed by my unwelcome attachment, moved the group away. I did hear her say, however, that most people flock to the Michelangelo *David*, which impresses everybody. Any idiot, any art-ignoramus (my interpretation of what she was saying) is impressed by the sheer magnitude of the piece. But the Donatello appeals to the true cognoscenti, who can see the genius of this work. Well, I told myself, maybe I don't qualify as an art expert, but I know what pleases me. And I like the Michelangelo.

Before returning to the hotel, I stopped to admire the Arno (River) again. I thought of the exquisite Puccini aria "O, Mio Babbino Caro," where the girl threatens to throw herself into the Arno. I sang it in my mind as I had actually done in one of our class recitals.

The highlight of the day was our scenic bus ride up to Fiesole. We passed incredibly beautiful gardens and estates. At some points of elevation, we could see Florence lying below us, resplendent in its majesty. At the restaurant all of my efforts at carefully avoiding calorie-laden foods came to naught. All my lost weight came back to me after that one meal. I ate with gusto several kinds of pasta, several kinds of meat, extra helpings of everything, and double portions of desserts. Ah, Woman, "thy name is gluttony."

Siena and Assisi: Tuesday, 30 June 1987

Today, leaving Florence we headed toward Siena. There I did the usual touristy things. I took pictures in the Campo, the piazza de-signed for civic events, including the Palio. Later we walked through the town past all kinds of interesting shops and up a hill until we reached the Duomo. The Duomo was not only refreshingly cool but also breathtakingly grand. I'm truly ashamed to admit that the first place I made a mad dash for was the Cappella di Santa Caterina. I'm ashamed because my motive for doing so was not nobly artistic: I simply wanted to see the mummified head of Santa Caterina again. I suppose many catholic churches revere relics of departed saints, but it seems the Italians surpass all others in their collection of and reverence for mummified pieces of fingers, heads, feet, and toes and complete bodies. To walk down the aisles of Italian cathedrals is to walk over the many resting saints buried beneath. I got a peculiar satisfaction out of seeing the puzzled expressions on the faces of the two Arab women as they sought to understand why anyone would want to preserve parts of human skeletons. Since I'm not catholic, I too have difficulty understanding such reverence. I do, however, try to keep an open mind and to avoid even an unconscious sneering.

If I was excited at the prospect of seeing Santa Caterina's head with Asmik and Hoda, I was practically straining at the leash to get to Assisi, where I could show them the <u>complete</u> body of Santa Chiara. I was inwardly (outwardly, too, I'm afraid) grinning with glee in anticipation of shocking Hoda and Asmik. I must admit that I was having a day of feeling anything but cultured. After all, how much constant erudition can a person stand at a stretch? After days and days of hearing about apses, sarcophagi, basilicas, catacombs, duomos, archaeological excavations, and the like, I felt that my cultural attention span just "got up and went." And the child in me had a good time marveling at the sacred body parts that hold the same fascination for me as do the Egyptian mummies. Unfortunately, I didn't get the chance to show this treat to the two Arab women.

Seriously, though, Assisi is beautiful. As the bus rounded the bend and permitted a first view of the Basilica di San Francesco, I caught my breath at the sight. On more sober reflection, however, I am disturbed at the grandeur of this monument to a saint who spurned this type of material splendor. It seems a mockery of the man himself— the humility he espoused, the poverty he embraced, the freedom of the soul he sought. The basilica is aesthetically awe-inspiring but evokes from me no feeling of sanctity. I view it in the same way I would any magnificent museum or any other work of architecture.

Spoleto: Thursday, 2 July 1987

How lovely to spend a birthday in such surroundings! I have developed a somewhat proprietary sense for this city. Since I had done a briefing of the city, as soon as the group entered the city, I felt that this was **my** city. As I pointed out some of the monuments I had talked about, I felt a sense of accomplishment as though I had built them or caused them to be. Studying a place helps us to know what we're looking at and to appreciate the richness of that particular culture.

I would have liked to spend several days in Spoleto in order to attend events in all of the monuments where the *Festival dei Due*

Mondi is held. This time I attended a performance of *Parsifal* in the Teatro Nuovo. On a previous trip to Spoleto, I had not paid particular attention to the acoustics. But, since I had recently read that those in this theater are especially resonant, I listened with a new appreciation for this theater. I would have enjoyed concerts at the Caio Melisso and at the Duomo. But there wasn't time enough.

I spent the whole day strolling around town and stopping at little bars to have *caffé latte decaffinato*. (The Italians referred generically to all decaffeinated coffee as "café ahgay" from *Kaffe Hague*, a brand name of a German decaffeinated coffee.). When I visited the city last year, I wasn't interested in trying the local specialties, but this time I tried one—gli strengazzi. The group and I talked with denizens of the town: waiters, a little old lady we met on the street, shopkeepers, etc. As we walked past the Teatro Nuovo, where *Parsifal* was scheduled for later that evening, we heard singers rehearsing for the night's performance.

We arrived early at the opera to get good seats because our gallery tickets weren't numbered. As we sat in joyful anticipation of the opera, a really strange thing happened. A very pretty young woman forced her way into our space, next to Ari. That was really odd because the gallery was almost empty. I was annoyed at being unnecessarily crowded. After a while, I felt completely unpleasant but made an effort to keep my annoyance from spoiling the evening for Ari. Yet I knew something was wrong about the situation. During Act II the girl moved over to sit by another guy. Within minutes they were holding hands and then left. It seems that the girl was looking to be picked up. But to sit through two acts of Wagner as a way of getting picked up seems a waste of time and money.

But back to the opera. We sat there riveted to the actions onstage. When I saw the director on television earlier that week, he seemed to be avant-garde. So I wondered whether he'd use any of the strange, distorted sexual interpretations that are so much in vogue today. I wondered whether he'd have any of his characters to relieve themselves of incredibly huge penises. God, how awful that such sights are forced upon an often unsuspecting audience! (Once in Frankfurt in an interpretation of *Macbeth* with Grace Bumbry as Lady Macbeth, the controversial Neuenfels shocked and offended our sensibilities by having one of the grooms castrate himself onstage. When the audience loudly protested, he yelled out, *"Arschloescher!"* ("Assholes.") However, though opportunities for such exploitation existed in the plot, this director handled the whole opera tastefully. There were a couple of scenes that appeared rather coarse. But thank goodness they stopped short of being obscene.

Parsifal still is not one of my favorite operas. And Wagner is not one of my favorite composers. However, it was a new and valuable experience for me. The briefing helped me to know what to look for and how to judge what I was experiencing. Because of this, I enjoyed the work much more than I would have if I had gone there cold.

Rome: Saturday, 4 July 1987

At the San Pietro Basilica today, my attention was immediately drawn to the unsightly, garish Baldacchino. It is incongruous to the rest of the Basilica, with the exception of the cathedral throne at the end of the apse. It detracts from the elegant simplicity of Michelangelo's cupola. The Baldacchino is an eyesore, which, if it must be tolerated, ought to be placed in an obscure area. As I try to appreciate it as an authentic piece in its own genre, I admit that its dimensions are awesome. Yet, if I were in charge of the place, I'd place this bit of incongruity with its "clowning cupids" and its garish green, twisting columns away from the serenely beautiful cupolas, which it stands under.

In a somber, pensive mood brought on by the solemnity of the surroundings; by a chorus of ancient holy women singing mass in voices sabotaged by age; by the *Pietà's* reminder of the tragedy of a Soul whose life's mission was to ease and eradicate human suffering and psychic ignorance—in such a mood I felt at once mournful and yet exuberant: mournful because of the suffering depicted in the

Pietà and exuberant because of the sheer beauty of the surroundings. As I sat there with conflicting emotions, I became aware of ethereal music wafting through the church. A choir was practicing. I experienced a few moments of ineffable joy as the choir sang, among other pieces, the "Ave Verum." Through the combination of that heavenly music reverberating over and over again and the aesthetic beauty of the Basilica, I briefly transcended the mundane world and merged into one harmonious whole with the spiritual. As I listened, I remembered the first time I had heard the "Ave Verum." (That was at LeMoyne College, where I was member of the Chancel choir under the direction of Prof. Whittaker.) As I listened this day, it was almost impossible to refrain from joining in the singing. In fact, a few notes did quietly escape despite my efforts to contain them.

As we later climbed the stairs to the dome, I felt that, whereas the music and the other art in the church had figuratively transported me to heaven, I was now literally on the way. In fact, some graffiti on one of the walls indicated this way "→ to heaven."

At the Castel Sant'Angelo, which we next visited, my overwhelming impression was one of horror and repulsion at the reminders of how cruel humans can be to one another. Appalling were the weapons of destruction, especially the swords, knives, and lances, whose blades were constructed not merely to kill but to eviscerate and tear out large pieces of human flesh. Then there were those inhumane holes in the ground, where humans condemned others of their own kind to relentless confinement, deprived of movement, of light, of sanity. Obviously, such cruelty was not relegated just to those times, those people, or those places. The Castel simply reminded me. It caused me to renew my efforts to eliminate traits within myself that could lead to acts of aggression—even such thoughts. Though we had not deliberately planned to visit the Castel on this day, how fitting that this visit to a former prison on Independence Day should be a reminder of how precious freedom is.

Rome, Tues., 7 July 1987

Until Hoda's briefing of *Aida*, I had not known that Verdi wrote the opera reluctantly. It was revealing to learn that great works of art are not always nobly or eagerly executed and to learn that Verdi's overriding concern was not that he was creating a masterpiece but that he was earning a lot of money. At any rate, *Aida* remains my favorite opera. It is the combination of the sensuously lush music full of tuneful arias; it is the story's setting, Egypt, the land of a people who have fascinated me since I first learned of their existence as a high school student; it is the physical grandeur that all the elements evoke; it is the story of a love given but not wanted and of another love forbidden because of politics, nationality, and social status.

Later in the evening I was so eager for the treat to begin that I arrived an hour early at the Terme di Caracalla. We had time to stroll about the grounds and to reflect on the former wealth and glory of the people who built these baths. The beautiful singing, the elaborate sets, the reminders of the ancient grandeur of the baths, the feeling of spaciousness due to the absence of walls—all combined to make me feel one with the universe of beauty.

Roma: Terme di Caracalla, Wed., 8 July 1987

Today's class made me think of how Socrates' classes might have been held: the class sitting around discussing and the teacher asking thought-provoking questions and encouraging the sharing of thoughts.

Yesterday's outing to the opera reminded me that some of my most pleasant times have been spent in or near baths. There are my personal baths, which I extend into a ritual of beauty and emotional regrouping as I luxuriate in a tub of perfumed, bubbly, steaming water. If I have the time or if I'm especially exhausted or if I want to celebrate being again in my own home after traveling, to the long, lazy soaking I add candle light. I sometimes include a glass of wine and soft music. If I really have lots of time, I might even take a magazine or a book. To me such a bath is a luxury I willingly bestow on myself. However, I try to be careful of the time I spend bathing in other people's homes. Last year, for example, I visited a friend in Egypt. There a brief excursion during which dust and perspiration were constant companions made me feel keenly the need of a bath. So, when I returned to the home of my host, I simply could not get out of the bath in less than an hour. I was very ashamed of myself and felt that I had not been a gracious guest, but I was powerless to resist the attractions of that bath.

Other pleasant times spent at baths include two events here in Rome: *Aida* at the Terme di Caracalla, ruins of once imperial baths dating from A.D. 212, and the class session today at Neptune's Bath in Ostia Antica, fourth-century ruins between the Tiber River and the Tyrrhenian Sea. In response to the instructor's request that we write our feelings of the day's event, I wrote the following.

Here as the class sat among the magnificent ruins, I experienced one of the loveliest days of my stay in Italy. In the spacious serenity of the surroundings, with birds singing and cool breezes wafting about us, I felt a harmony I had not felt before with this group. There was a genuine sharing of ideas by everyone present. It was as if the instructor transcended the typical role of a person imparting knowledge to a passive group and became a part of the beauty that results when knowledge-seekers find their own. It was a group of well-informed people, adventurous, eager to know; a group appreciative of the grandeur and accomplishments of past ages; a group sensitive to the ideas and views of others; and a group grateful to those others for their various experiences and for their willingness to share those experiences by which we vicariously see places and do things. As we "broke bread together" while discussing art, music, architecture, I realized fully the metaphor of the etymology of the word "company," someone to whom we feel close enough to have bread (food) with.

CHAPTER XI

Non-European Reactions to My Kind

I t is strange but foreigners often are drawn to Audrey and me. People from various parts of the earth sometimes seek us out to befriend us. For example, on the *QE2* one of the dining room stewards, a young Brit, became so friendly that he told us about his Caribbean girlfriend. Once he was so engrossed in talking about missing her that he actually sat down at our table. After a few minutes, his cell phone rang. After listening to the voice on the other end, he quickly left our table and resumed his post. We assumed that the maitre d' or some other higher-up had taken him to task for fraternizing with the passengers. He never did it again.

In Palma de Majorca, Audrey and I were attending TESL classes with Trenton State (now the College of New Jersey). Of the educators and housewives from many countries, Audrey and I were the only two African Americans. The class included two women from Pakistan and a Middle Eastern housewife, who invited us to dinner at her apartment there on the island. All three were well-to-do and invited us to visit them in their countries. Although we were from differing cultures, we were all very relaxed with one other. Audrey has a personality that draws people to her, and I am approachable.

On a quiet evening in the restaurant of the Tunisian Hilton, a waiter joined us at our table and told us things about the city. He also pointed out the party of Mrs. Arafat, who was dining across the room from us.

Once in a downtown department store in Frankfurt, Audrey, Sadie, and I noticed a brown-skinned salesclerk. Germany had just begun to hire people of color as salesclerks, so Lashini was enough of a novelty to draw our notice. Naturally Audrey, the friendly one, was sent to meet the clerk. We found out that she was South African of Indian descent and that she was married to a German. Later Sadie invited Lashini and her mother to tea at Sadie's. Eagerly joining the conversation, the mother said that she felt more relaxed then than at any other time during her visit to Germany because we looked like many of the people in their homeland of Durban, South Africa.

Then in the *Inlingua* language school, there was our own mini-United Nations consisting of Ninfa, a tiny Peruvian married to a German she had met in Peru; Laura, a gregarious post-teen from Columbia; "Fiji," a brown, curly-haired Fijian cohabiting with her possessive German jailor and his controlling mother; Trina, a beauty who had fled Afghanistan along with some members of her aristocratic family; Pierre, a handsome, rather shy lawyer from France; Bob, our Scottish-American friend who taught at the language school; and Audrey and me, two very friendly African Americans.

As hard as it might be to believe, there was a tiny moment when Trina and I competed for Pierre's attentions. Well, not really competed because Pierre was married and displayed no romantic notions toward either of us. Also, I think he was absolutely baffled by the antics of fully grown, educated, professional women who reverted to child-like behavior when they got together. Once in the language class we tried to divert the teacher's attention as Trina crept around on the floor, trying to be inconspicuous as she took a note to someone in the class. Another time when we were in my car, I teasingly offered to take Pierre for a rendezvous in the woods we were passing. Looking back on those times, I see that we were absolutely ridiculous, but we had such fun!

Sometimes the group would come to my place for a home-cooked dinner. Once we met at a restaurant. Always we had a marvelous time. There was a moment when I felt a tiny stab of envy toward Trina. At the restaurant she had managed to get a seat next to Pierre. For a while after that, her abundant dark hair reminded me of a Persian cat, all hairy and fuzzy. (I don't like cats.)

She later married a rich German art dealer and lived in a gorgeous apartment in Germany. Years later, Audrey saw her again, divorced, fabulous, and living in luxury in England. She never knew that I envied her beauty. I hope she never reads these memoirs.

I don't know whether our good relations with foreigners result from our friendliness, but we jokingly say that it is the warmth radiating from our brown skin. Seriously, I do think that skin color has something to do with the ease that some foreigners have in our company: many of them are people of color, too. And I think that the color bespeaks a kind of kinship in a world ruled by white skin.

Actually, it's not the skin's color but what it represents. When people see us, they don't see the "average American," the stereotypical Caucasian who feels superior to everyone else; who really believes that all other races are created to do his bidding, to serve him. When they see us, these foreigners see people whose color, like theirs, marks them as being considered not quite worthy of the respect and consideration given to possessors of white skin. Both East Indians and Egyptians have told me that when the British and other Caucasians occupied their lands, the occupiers regarded the indigenous (dark) people as inferiors.

Still, there have been instances where being the possessor of brown skin (something I have absolutely nothing to do with) has had its tiny rewards. Sometimes people have allowed me certain pleasantries denied to others. On one occasion Peggy, an African American oboist with the Hessischer Rundfunk Orchestra, and I went to Milan to see a performance at the world-famous La Scala. When we arrived at the opera house, we found that there were no tickets for sale. Completely disappointed after having spent hours on the train to Milan and money for a hotel room, we stood outside with the other opera-goers in the same situation. A few minutes before the opera began, one of the ushers came out, looked over the crowd, spotted us, and handed us free tickets for the night's performance. Why did he choose us? He didn't say; he simply handed us the tickets and left. Whatever the reason, we were grateful for this unexpected gift. The opera, Verdi's *I Lombardi,* unfamiliar to me, was not one of my favorites. But that didn't matter. What did matter was that after living in Europe for years, I was finally able to attend a performance at La Scala.

Another occasion when I was the recipient of an unexpected favor happened in southern Spain. One afternoon, I stopped by a hotel to have lunch. Not realizing that I had come at off hours (after lunch and before dinner), I ordered a hot meal. When the waiter brought the meal, he allowed me to eat it on the balcony. As I sat there enjoying my meal and the view, a woman of European descent came into the dining room and tried to order a hot meal. The waiter told her that the dining room was closed until dinner time but that she could have a sandwich. When she asked whether she could eat it outside, he told her that the balcony was also closed until dinner time. So I sat there feeling a bit guilty as the woman sat in the dining room eating her cold sandwich. However, such occasions counterbalanced the unpleasantries I sometimes encountered—for example, the moppet in Spoleto, who sitting on her father's shoulders, spotted me in the crowd, pointed, and yelled: "*Fea! Fea!*" ("Ugly! Ugly!").

CHAPTER XII

German Reactions

Whereas the southern Europeans regarded me as an exotic entity, many Germans looked at me as a distant relative of ET's. They seemed surprised that my mundane actions were exactly like theirs—for example, that I ate with knife, fork, and spoon.

In 1972, soon after I arrived for the first time in Germany, three African American female friends and I had lunch in the restaurant of a downtown department store, the *Kaufhof*. As we sat there eating our lunch, there was silence as all eyes were on us. It was like performing in a theater in the round. All eyes followed our every movement. When one of us spoke, German eyes focused on that person. When another of us responded, German attention shifted to that speaker. When one of us raised a fork, eyes watched its progress all the way to the diner's lips.

Other examples occurred at the opera. During intermission, a German friend and I often joined the crowd in the foyer for a cigarette and a glass of wine. Waiting for the next act to begin, the crowd would stroll along the room. When they reached us, they would lose their stride, do a double take, and almost trip over their own feet.

Noticing the confusion, my friend would ask, "What are they looking at?" I knew only too well.

Another friend and I were driving along the Autobahn. Cars whizzing by slowed up so that the occupants could get a good look into our car. Uli too wondered, "Why are they staring so?"

As ET's cousin, I could count on having plenty of seat space on public transportation. Only as a last resort did the passengers looking for seats choose the one next to me. Actually, that was quite nice: I've always wanted lots of space.

I have never really understood how people in a modern country like Germany could be so astounded by the sight of an African American going about the everyday business of living. After all, there were thousands of Americans in Germany at that time, and many were African American. I think it might have been the fact that Americans were seldom seen outside the military areas: the PX, the commissary, the American movie houses, the housing areas. So as my friends and I moved about on the economy (that's what we called the German sections that had nothing to do with the American military), I guess we were indeed rare sights.

Not all Germans were callous and murderous like those who committed those heinous acts against the "undesirables" after the fall of communism. Most of the ones that I had contact with were decent people. In fact, in Kronberg am Taunus, Herr and Frau Rörig were the best neighbors I could hope for. To me they were like beloved relatives: helpful yet unobtrusive. I knew that they would come to my aid if needed, yet they never pried. We were so close that the wife had a key to my apartment and periodically would come in to feed my tropical fishes and even to clean the fish tank. Though I lived alone in the apartment, I lived in the security of knowing that the Rörigs were right across the hall.

Then there were my church members. From the time I first entered the Reading Room of the Second Church of Christ, Scientist, I felt the warmth and acceptance of most of the members. I say "most" intentionally. Not all received me with open arms and hearts. There was a seven-year-old boy who was absolutely terrified of me. Though I had said nothing to him, his eyes bulged in fright whenever he saw me in church. Once his mother and grandmother invited me to their home for an evening meal. The poor little boy was petrified. He hung onto his mother the whole time I was there, much to the chagrin of the mother and grandmother. I've had people look at me with animosity but never before with a terror that rendered them mute.

Contrary to these negative reactions to me, to the Germans in the Frankfurt German American Community Choir, there was only oneness. Just as a symphony is a blending of many different instruments to produce one whole, so was it with our choir. When we sang, there was no concern with nationality, race, or skin color. The only color of importance was the timbre, the color of the voice/instrument. When we were not singing but relaxing and socializing, seldom did our nationality or race enter into our times together. If we grouped according to any principle, it was not nationality but the sections to which our tonal range assigned us: sopranos with sopranos, altos with altos, tenors with tenors, and basses with basses. Shortly before a concert, the choir would have a weekend retreat at the Familienferienstätte Dortweil, outside Schmitten in the Taunus Mountains. There we spent most of the time rehearsing for the upcoming concert. But we had breaks during which we could drive down the mountain and back to the city or to the nearby village or just relax. At the end of the day, we would meet in the bar for wine, beer, snacks, and—incredibly—more singing that often lasted unto midnight. It was a time of a joy that was spiritual, one based on the music and the fellowship.

To paraphrase Saint Paul, there was neither German nor American, neither black nor white. We were **one** with the music and the others.

CHAPTER XIII

Conflicts of Cultures: Gestures and Other Strange Behavior

B efore going to Europe and living among nationalities other than American, I hadn't realized that gestures were not universal. For example, we beckon someone to us by stretching the arm out with the palm facing us and waving the fingers toward ourselves. Conversely, Italians (and perhaps other cultures) beckon by stretching the arm out, the palm of the hand toward the other person, and waving the fingers up and down—a signal that to us means to go away. On one occasion when I asked an Italian woman for directions, she began her "backward" wave, so I started to walk away. But she waved ever more furiously until I realized that she was signaling me to come toward her. After much starting forward and then backward, I finally understood that I was to follow her.

Another gesture (one that could prove dangerous) is the two-finger sign. In London, two American friends told a bus conductor that they wanted two tickets. Evidently, there was some confusion (maybe accent problems), so Evelyn, one of the women, clarified the number wanted by raising two fingers with the backside of the hand toward the conductor. As he looked at her in astonishment, she kept gesturing with her fingers and saying, "But I want only two!" Recovering from his shock, the conductor said, "Love, that is rude."

In Germany, an East Indian couple used to attend the chapel on the military installation where I taught. I don't know how long they had been a part of the American culture, but they hadn't yet mastered its conventions. To Americans, shaking the head from side to side means "no." To the Indians, it means "yes." To us, nodding the head means "yes," but to them it means "no." When asked whether she had enjoyed the services, the poor wife would sometimes get so confused as she sought the gesture that would convey her meaning that she would start out with a nod and then switch to a shake and then back to a nod. I found it amusing—until I thought of similar situations in which I had made myself look completely ridiculous.

An occasion, not of odd gestures, but of strange and thoroughly disgusting behavior, involves a matter of hygiene. My friends always laughed at my fastidiousness in not drinking after others; in waiting for someone else to open doors of public toilets after I had washed my hands; in refusing food handled by naked, unwashed hands; in not letting people put their hands into my bags of snacks; and in detesting the habit of wetting one's fingers with saliva and then touching my items. So all the more ironic was the situation with a guy from Ghana .One day C. arrived unexpectedly at my apartment in Germany. (Some months earlier, for half a day I had been his house guest in Greece, where he was studying at a university.) He had bought a used car and driven from Greece to Germany because he was eager to meet some of my American friends. At the end of his week-long visit, he said he couldn't find my hair brush. When I asked whether he had been using my hairbrush, he replied, "Yes, and your toothbrush, too." Ugh!

Once when I was on a bus tour in southern Italy, across the aisle sat a young South American with whom I'd been having a pleasant conversation. At a quick stop, I bought a large bottle of soda pop and looked forward to drinking it on the bus. As I prepared to drink it, the young man asked to take a sip and reached for the bottle. Of course, I refused—politely. Misunderstanding the reason for my refusal, he said he wanted only a little bit of the soda. This time refusing firmly, I explained that I didn't allow people to drink from containers that I was using. (His drinking from the bottle would have spoiled all of the contents, for I had no intentions of drinking the soda after he had put his lips on the mouth of the bottle and possibly had let a little of the soda dribble back into the bottle.) He actually became offended by my refusal and said no more to me during the rest of the tour. Did I care? I looked at the scenery, read my book, and drank my soda in peace, the whole refreshing bottleful.

Another time there was no way to refuse without offending someone who had been very kind to me. One Wednesday night after school was over and my chores were done, on my way to church services I bought a favorite yoghurt drink to enjoy in the few minutes before services started. I had been very busy that day and hadn't had time to eat, so I was looking forward to that drink, which would have appeased my hunger until I arrived home an hour and a half later. As I put the straw to my lips, one of the German women (kind of an official of the church) came over, took the bottle from my hands, and took a big sip from my straw! Well, that did it! Diplomacy required that I say nothing. But I was furious! I gathered my things and left before church started. Outside, I threw the container into the trash bin, and fuming, drove home.

Sometimes the French carry long loaves of unwrapped baguettes under their arms. If they have to ride the streetcar, they place the unwrapped bread on the overhead racks. Not for me, this habit. In all fairness, I'm sure that Europeans and others find some of our American ways utterly illogical.

A misinterpretation of body language can not only be annoying but also get a person into a lot of trouble. The traveler to a foreign land needs to know as much as possible about the actions that the people consider socially and morally unacceptable. It is unwise to take one's customs to a foreign country and to expect the people to adapt to them. To do so can lead to dire consequences. I remember reading of a case where an American girl was killed by a foreigner who mistook her friendliness for romantic interest. Because she had on occasion smiled at him, he interpreted that action as an invitation to a relationship. When she refused his attentions, he killed her as a matter of honor for her "having led him on." He had brought to America some cultural mores that were totally out of place here. He obviously had not sufficiently studied the American people and their customs.

Of course, nothing so devastating happened to me, but in my travels I did sometimes take with me a certain amount of ignorance of the people and their customs. Although I had knowledge of some languages and some monuments, I knew little about the people themselves. Therefore, I found myself committing some egregious breaches of propriety.

For example, on one trip to Cairo, an Egyptian friend and I were seated with some friends at a sidewalk café. The group included an Italian girl I had met on the ferry from Italy and an Egyptian couple. To make a point during the conversation, I reached over and touched my friend on his naked thigh. (He was wearing shorts.) There was an audible gasp from the Egyptian woman. Not realizing that I had just committed a faux pas, I continued to touch him as we talked. Shortly afterward, as the couple took leave of us, the wife shook the hands of my guy and the Italian woman. Not looking once in my direction, she ignored me completely. Later, I found that my actions had branded me as a woman of "questionable morals." According to her customs, I was a bold hussy publicly conveying a sexual desire for my guy.

On another occasion (this time in Alexandria), the same Italian girl and I were at a seaside café one evening. The manager of the bar spoke English, so we were having an enjoyable conversation. Then a married couple joined the group. Though the husband spoke English, the wife didn't. Therefore, not being able to understand what was being said, she had to rely on what was being done (or what she thought was occurring). As we laughed and talked, the Italian girl touched the husband's arm. The wife, until then silent, let loose a volley of angry-sounding words and offered her purse to the Italian girl. Because touching had a sexual connotation in that culture, the wife thought that we were ladies of the night and that the Italian girl had just propositioned her husband.

Another time, wearing jeans and sandals with a slight heel, I walked down a Cairo sidewalk. Suddenly, a group of teenage girls started shouting at me and mimicking my walk. I was angry: my shoe strap had just broken, it was hot, and I was tired of being harassed as I innocently tried to enjoy the scenery. The girls shouted and I shouted, neither of us understanding the heated words being spoken but understanding the intent. If I had not been rescued by a man passing by, there might have been an international incident. Later an Egyptian friend described my walk as a kind of dance. Yet, it was simply the walk of the Western woman, who moves freely without conscious thought of being considered provocative. And then there was the matter of jeans. I had been told that wearing jeans was now permissible, provided that they were not too tight. On a Cairo tram, whenever the tram swerved, the man who sat across from me ever so slightly touched my jeans-clad knee. After a few instances of this **accidental** touching, I said in an audible voice: "Do you have enough room?" He sat back and mumbled something by way of apology (I guess). I don't know that he understood English, but a leave-me-alone message is probably universally understood.

CHAPTER XIV

Forgotten Passports and
Lost Trains and Buses

Wher traveling in Europe, next in importance after money, medication, and eyeglasses is the **passport.** Without it, a person could be stuck in limbo.

On one occasion, when I had joined my cousin Hazel in Torremolinas, her tour group was scheduled to sail from Malaga, Spain, to Tangier, Morocco. When we arrived at the port, I realized that I had left my passport in Hazel's hotel room, where I had spent the night in order to be on time. (Since I was not a member of the Chicago tour group, I was staying at a less expensive hotel nearby and was traveling with the group to Morocco.) A young African American found that he, too, had left his passport. Of course, the ship sailed without us.

The two of us returned to the hotel, got our passports, and took a bus to the coastal city of Algeciras. From there we took a ferry to Morocco. After many hours, we arrived in Tangier. Although I didn't know the name of the hotel, I wasn't worried: my fellow passportforgetter assured me that he did. In the taxi, when I asked the hotel's name, he said: "Luxus." **Luxus?** He had given me not the name, but the category: "Deluxe." There we were, two Americans in a foreign country seeking our friends in a hotel whose name we did not know. What to do? Crying (a common recourse among travelers in similar circumstances) wouldn't have helped. From the taxi driver we learned that there were only four hotels that catered to such groups as ours and that for a small fee he would take us to all four. Luckily, at the second hotel, we looked at passport photos of the hotel guests and recognized our group. Finally, several hours after the group had left Malaga, I knocked on my cousin's door.

Another occasion of a forgotten passport was the time I went to Budapest with my friend Bob, a Scottish-American living in Germany. We met up at the Frankfurt train station, where I discovered that I had left my passport at home. Thankfully, the train station was close enough that I could take public transportation to go home to get the passport.

This was not the most pleasant of trips. Budapest itself was unattractive. It was midwinter and the city was hidden under layers of dirty snow. And simple things like Kleenex, soap, and toilet tissue were difficult to obtain. Bob and I stayed at a government-sponsored home of a couple who took in travelers. One day after sightseeing, I was tired and wanted to return to our lodgings, but Bob wanted to explore the city. Feeling overly confident, I took a tram and followed landmarks to the corner where I was supposed to get off. As usual, my observations had not been exact enough. I was at the correct corner but didn't know which direction to take. Street signs? Written all in Magyar, a branch of the Finno-Ugric language family, they were completely useless to me. I couldn't ask passersby because I didn't know a single word of their language, and I was sure that the average person on the street didn't know English. What to do? I didn't know. As I stood there on the verge of tears, I saw my savior Bob coming down the street. He had decided to go in early, also. Since he knew the way, we soon arrived at the house, where we spent a pleasant time talking with the couple, who were quite hospitable. The wife found English to be exotic and elegant. We assumed that they were members of the Communist Party because the home had modern conveniences, the wife had perfumes and tissues (luxury items), and they dressed in glamorous evening wear for some event they attended. In total contrast were a former university professor and his wife. They had been reduced to living in one room, which was so devoid of amenities that the one thing the wife asked us to send from the West was a can opener. At that time, Bob was a language teacher at *Inlingua Sprachschule* in Frankfurt, and friends had given him names of people to contact in Budapest. Another professor/student asked me to mail him a copy of *Gulag Archipelago*, which was not available in the East. After I returned to Germany, I sent him the book. A few days later, the book was returned to me. Thinking no ill, I sent it back, and again it was returned to me. By then, I realized that the book was forbidden. Fearful of causing an international event, I didn't send it again. We never heard from the person who had asked me to send it, but my imagination created all sorts of distressing scenarios.

On our way back to West Germany and still in Soviet territory, we noticed an elderly man being rudely spoken to. Though he had a ticket for a sleeping car, the conductor refused to allow him to move from the open coach. Elderly people were allowed to leave the communist countries but were ill-treated when they did. I felt sorrow at seeing that venerable man treated so disrespectfully. Of course, we remained silent: we were, after all, Americans in hostile territory.

Years later, when I revisited Budapest during a summer, the whole city had undergone a metamorphosis. It was beautiful. Across the Danube, we could see Buda, the modern city on the west bank, and Pest, the older, on the east. Both parts were impressive, but the more modern Buda had many high end shops that rivaled those of Paris, New York, Milan, and London. Pest, on the other hand, had magnificent buildings from the past and an old-world flavor.

In Barcelona, the setting for another of my mishaps, I lost, not a passport, but a whole tour bus. After traveling frugally for some days,

I allowed myself the pleasure of a guided tour to Montserrat, the mountain site of the Benedictine monastery, which houses one of the many Black Madonnas of Europe. After visiting some of the sights of the saw-toothed mountain, I headed to the restaurant where the group was scheduled to have lunch. I found the restaurant but not the group. After looking around frantically for several minutes and not finding the group on the first floor as scheduled, I tried to find the bus. Well, there must have been a hundred buses on top of that mountain, and I hadn't noted our spot. Then I stood outside and looked at passersby to see whether I could recognize anyone. (I now empathize with Caucasians who say that we all look alike to them.) I am ashamed to say that I had the same thought. On a bus full of unfamiliar Caucasians, I had failed to note particular characteristics. And now, hundreds of pale faces were passing in front of me. And they all truly **did** look alike to me. So there I was: atop a mountain with no way to get down and back to my hotel 36 miles away; hungry and unable to find the lunch for which I had splurged; and recognizing no one in that ocean of paleness. Fighting back tears, I finally recognized the blond pony tail of a woman who had been sitting several seats in front of me. Eagerly, I ran to her. She gave me directions to the bus and reminded me that the Europeans' first floor was our second (their ground floor not counting as part of the numbering). I had found the right restaurant, and the lunch was indeed on the first floor but upstairs on what we call the **second** floor.

Since I still had time, I returned and ordered my meal. Of course, I spoke in a Spanish broken even more by the ordeal I had just undergone. The amazing thing was that the waiter not only understood me but complimented me on my intelligence in speaking Spanish. **Intelligence?** In someone who had just lost a whole tour bus and a restaurant floor; who had lost a whole train on a Scandinavian ferry; who had left her passport in a hotel in Torremolinos while en route to Morocco; who had lost a whole bed and breakfast place in Budapest? Intelligence? As Eliza Doolittle says: "Not bloody likely."

CHAPTER XV

European Toilets

A must in any memoir of Europe is a discussion of that blight on civilized living—the European toilet. Though on occasion, a reference to the waxed-paper consistency of Europe's toilet tissue can be found, I have never seen a discussion of the toilet itself. Perhaps that is due to its extremely private function. However, that function is vital to our well-being, and its urgency (as Julius Caesar says about death) "will come when it will come." Thus, information on this delicate topic is no less necessary than that on how to find the train station, the library, and the hospital.

The typical European toilet bears little resemblance to the American toilet. It is not a toilet (commode) but a hole carved into the floor and surrounded on either side by footprints inset into the floor. For the lucky users, there will be some kind of rack to hold on to. When there is no supporting rack, a person needs to have a dancer's balance to be able to squat over the hole. Woe to the woman wearing slacks during a certain time of the month. She has to hold the pants legs up high enough to avoid their touching the mess below. At the same time, she has to be careful not to allow any menstrual fluid to drip onto her slacks—all the while trying to make sure she doesn't fall on her naked bottom into the cesspool. I guess the European woman has mastered the art: I've never heard otherwise. For the unfortunate American tourist? It's a *tour de force*.

Since I lived in modern Frankfurt, Germany, I had given little thought to toilets. The first place I experienced this phenomenon was a *pension* in Paris. After a while, searching for a regular toilet with a seat, I went to a cinema—only to discover the same type of toilet. The West German bathrooms are much more advanced than those of the French. In Germany, only in the remotest areas can such toilets be found. Most establishments and homes have toilets like the American ones. Some of them, though, are flushed by pulling a long chain extending from the tank, which is near the ceiling.

Ah, but it gets worse. Once, outside a *souk* (bazaar) in Turkey, Audrey, Sadie, and I looked for a toilet. There was one, but it had no seat. I paid the required equivalent of fifty cents to rent a seat. As a matter of principle, Sadie refused to do so, adding instead the fifty cents to the 200 dollars she spent for jewelry she bought in the same bazaar. Another time, after a very long train ride from Frankfurt, Sadie and I arrived in Brindisi, Italy. Among the things we desperately needed were a toilet and a hot shower. Two makeshift shower stalls were inside an outdoor structure. Hot water was to be found only in the one for men. The owner was so impressed by my feeble attempts to speak Italian that he allowed **me** to use the one with the hot water. But the toilet! No seat—not even one to be rented. What to do? When in Rome....It's amazing how quickly we can adapt when we must.

In a lovely hotel overlooking Lake Baikal in Siberia, the bathroom looked clean and inviting. However, whereas in the Western World, the trash can is a receptacle for, among other things, used paper towels, in this hotel it was a receptacle for used toilet paper. Need I explain? The toilet in the airport in Vladivostok, Siberia, was the worst I've ever encountered. In addition to a far-ranging stench, this toilet was the typical hole-in-the-floor type, this time with puddles of urine dating from the Stalin era.

In Muslim countries and on some Greek ferries, toilet paper is not a standard. Instead, there is a hose-like tube through which water flows and, along with the left hand, is used to rinse the private parts. I visited a family in Egypt and, noticing the absence of toilet paper, used my stash of Kleenex as long as it lasted. Finally, I asked the hostess where I could buy toilet paper. She apologized and said that she had forgotten that we (Westerners) used toilet paper. I was surprised that the corner grocery store actually had an ample supply of toilet tissue. How could there be enough of a demand in Cairo for stores to stock such?

Another difference is the European and Asian structure known as a *bidet*, which is unfamiliar to most Americans. In fact, instead of using it for the purpose for which it was designed (the washing of one's nether regions), some Americans in Thailand used theirs to wash clothes.

In toilets in Budapest restaurants we visited, there was no free access to toilet paper in the stalls. An attendant doled out two or three squares to a customer. Woe to the unfortunate cold-sufferer with a nose full of mucus! I learned to keep lots of Kleenex with me at all times.

God bless America for hot water, flushing toilets, toilet seats, plenty of non-lacerating toilet paper, deep bath tubs, roomy shower stalls, and fluffy bath towels.

CHAPTER XVI

American Unfavorable Impressions

I fear that on two occasions I unintentionally left behind bad impressions of Americans. Both involved train travel.

School was out and my friend Mary, a school nurse, and I were on our way to Perugia to spend a month studying Italian. We were excited as only school personnel can be when summer comes and we shed our disciplinarians' hats to be who we were really are: travelers, students, and enjoyers of life. From Frankfurt, we traveled to Munich, where we would change trains. Since it seemed that we had a lot of time between trains, we ordered breakfast in Munich's station café. When we only were halfway through our meal, we heard the conductor announcing the arrival and imminent departure of our connecting train. Having only a few minutes to get to the train, we jumped up, grabbed our things, and, forgetting the unpaid waitress, ran for our train. We didn't think of her until the next day, when we were in Perugia. Of course we felt awful; we hadn't meant to cheat her, but, since we didn't know her name, we couldn't send the money to her. For months afterward, I wanted to do something. I even thought of going to Munich to find her and pay the money. That was a very impractical idea because it would have been costly, time-consuming, and probably futile to look for someone I wouldn't have recognized.

Another summer, part of my travel through Spain was on the luxury train, the *Talgo*. Since I was traveling with a Eurail pass, I had first class accommodations. One of the amenities offered by this train was the opportunity for first-class passengers to have a real, restaurant-class hot meal. So I ordered a delicious lunch. I noticed that some diners placed their empty trays into the racks on the back of the seats in front. After doing the same when I finished, I went to the washroom. When I returned I thought nothing of the fact that my tray had been taken away and that no one asked for pay. It never occurred to me that I was expected to pay: I assumed naively that a free meal was one of the amenities of first-class travel. (I'm still not sure, but I think the person collecting the trays assumed that I had paid before going to the washroom.) At any rate no one said anything, and I didn't think of it until years later. It remains one of those things I wish I could make right.

CHAPTER XVII

Ireland at Last

In my undergrad years, I sometimes heard Dennis Day, an Irish American tenor, sing Irish songs so full of longing that they haunted me for years, so much so that I promised myself a visit to Ireland one day. My being so moved by Irish songs was unexplainable, for, in my segregated, black world of Memphis, Tennessee, I had never met anyone who had even the slightest acquaintance with Ireland. Still, the deep sadness in those songs elicited a heartfelt response from me. Yet I would be in Europe twenty years before crossing the Celtic Sea to Ireland.

One summer I traveled by train and ship to Youghal in County Cork to visit my friend Mary, a school nurse with DoDDS Germany. Mary had two homes in Ireland: the family home in the process of being renovated and a small estate she owned with her daughter and son-in-law. When I arrived, Mary led me to my portion of the baronial house, the second floor, which contained a state-of-the art-bathroom, a library with a fireplace, several rooms, and a bedroom with a view of the distant sea. Mary was always a classy lady: once on a train trip to Italy, she brought along small candles, cloth napkins, and wine for our basket lunch in the coach. In Ireland it was the same: she had equipped my room with antique lace bed linens and had left for me the books *The Famine* and *Trinity*, whose themes are the Great Potato Famine and the struggle for Irish independence.

True to reports, Ireland has a beauty enhanced by very green land and blue seas. The pathos that I associate with Ireland results from the seemingly endless rainfall and the harshness of a land so filled with stones in some parts that raising crops is almost impossible. Yet it is a beautiful land. On a bus tour one day, I was moved to tears by the beauty of the place, by its sad history, and by the warmth of the people. With the soft sounds of the gentle rain and the haunting sounds of the driver's cd's featuring the Irish harp, it was impossible not to be moved.

I visited many cities: among them Limerick, Dublin (where I stayed in a dormitory of a college closed for the holidays), and Galway. From Galway City I took a ferry to Inis Oirr, one of the Aran Islands. The guide books aptly describe the Aran Islands as "rugged and barren." The islands' remoteness seems both geographical and social. It is like a return to the past and deliberately so, I read. Though there are bed and breakfast lodgings with modern amenities, the place seems rooted in the past. I didn't find much to do there other than to admire the unfamiliar terrain and the stillness. Of the many places I have visited, the Aran Islands seem the most isolated from modernity.

Of all the nations I have met, the Irish on the whole are the nicest. They are very warm, accommodating people. Early one morning I waited in a café for the tour bus to arrive. When the café opened service, I ordered tea and scones. Almost as soon as I began the small meal, the bus arrived. Being certain that we had to leave then, I started to get up, but the driver told me that I could finish. He actually waited until I had finished my meal! Never in America, never in Germany, never in Greece, and never in any other country!

CHAPTER XVIII

Aufwiedersehen, DoDDS Germany

As civilians, teachers had a status equal to that of Colonel. Though we worked and lived with the military, we were not **in** the military. In my years in Frankfurt, I was immersed in the world of the military personnel: I taught their children, I had parent-teacher conferences with them, I sang with them, I shopped with them, and I visited their homes. Everyday I saw military uniforms. Yet it was with Operation Desert Storm in 1990 that I began consciously to connect the people I saw daily with the actuality of war, of killing and being killed.

In the Annex (the 2-story building where I taught), we had to move all classrooms from the second floor in order to make room to house the soldiers coming in to ship out for Desert Storm. The building where I taught was located near the guarded entry to the post. From my classroom windows, I could see tanks rolling in. As I took cookies and magazines to soldiers lying on make-shift beds on the second floor, the expressions on their faces told me that this was what the military meant: the very real possibility of being killed in battle. For the first time I realized that some of my seniors who were going off to West Point and other military academies were preparing for not just a career but the eventuality of war; that these fresh-faced, innocent, eager young men and women just beginning adulthood probably had not thought of the military as anything more than a career. For most of their young lives, America had been relatively free of wars. Now loomed the prospect of their being killed or injured in a war.

After the fall of Communism in 1989 and the subsequent dismantling of the Berlin Wall, it was decided that a foreign military force of its present size was no longer necessary in Europe. Therefore, the military began a series of base closings and prepared to turn certain areas over to the Europeans. Our compound was one. In this drawdown, sometimes families were split as personnel were reassigned to one base and their military spouses to another in perhaps a different country. Long-established friendships were geographically split. After having lived in one place for many years, some people decided to retire instead of starting over in another location.

Shortly afterward, I said goodbye to DoDDS, the best career situation I have ever had. Though I am happy to be back in my own country, where we experience a freedom unimaginable in many places, I will always be thankful to God for allowing me to live, work, and travel in Europe.

I sometimes think of my European experience with longing, yet I am thankful for the blessings I have received since my return to the States in 1995. Best of all is that I have watched my brother's oldest child Dedara grow from an in-charge older sister to a member of the education profession, his son Andre from a mischievous boy to a happily married man, and his youngest child Pam from an inquisitive five-month-old to an independent college student. While teaching as an adjunct instructor of English at Camden County College, I have become computer literate enough to write these memoirs. I have met wonderful people and made new friends. After living "out of a suitcase" for twenty-three years, I now have a measure of stability and my own home, which I can furnish to my own taste.

Appendix 1

European and North African Waters I Have Crossed

Body of Water	From	To
Adriatic Sea	Ancona, Italy	Alexandria, Egypt
Aegean Sea	Greek Isles	Greek Isles
Celtic Sea	France	Cork, Ireland
Cretan Sea	Piraeus, Greece	Heraklion, Crete
English Channel	Dieppe, France	Folkstone, England
Ionian Sea	Brindisi, Italy	Patras, Greece
Mediterranean Sea	Algeciras, Spain	Tangier, Morocco
Mediterranean Sea	Barcelona, Spain	Palma de Mallorca
Mediterranean Sea (Gulf of Tunis)	Genoa, Italy	Tunis, Tunisia

North Sea (Strait of Dover)	Ostende, Belgium	Dover, England
Norwegian Sea	Lofoten Islands	Bergen, Norway
Tyrrhenian Sea	Reggio Calabria, Italy	Siracusa, Sicily
Atlanta Ocean	Southampton, England	New York, New York and back to Southampton

*The following sailings took place before I left for Europe in 1972.

Caribbean Sea	New York, New York	San Juan, Martinique, Curacao, St. Thomas, and Kingston
Caribbean Sea	New York, New York	Bahamas

the author on left and COUSIN Hazel aboard the S.S. Olympia

the author (with eyeglasses) and Geraldine Purnell aboard ship

the author and Geraldine at safety drill

the author in the late 70s